THE BEST HOMES

from

This Old House®

THE BEST HOMES
from
This Old House®

Kevin O'Connor
host of the Emmy-winning series

photographs by Michael Casey

STEWART, TABORI & CHANG
NEW YORK

For Kathleen.
You took care of everything else while I took care of this. Thank you.

For my beautiful girls, Lisa and Riley.
Your smiles and enthusiastic support got me through. Love you.

Stewart, Tabori & Chang | New York
Published in 2011 by Stewart, Tabori & Chang
An imprint of ABRAMS

Library of Congress Cataloging-in-Publication Data

O'Connor, Kevin (Kevin Douglas)
  The best homes from This old house / by Kevin O'Connor ; photographs by
Michael Casey.
    p. cm.
  Includes index.
  ISBN 978-1-58479-935-1
  1. Dwellings—Remodeling—United States. 2. Dwellings—United
States—Maintenance and repair. 3. Architecture, Domestic—United States.
I. Casey, Michael (Michael William) II. This old house (Television program)
III. Title.
  TH4816.O29 2011
  643'.7—dc23
                    2011018212

Editor: Dervla Kelly
Designer: LeAnna Weller Smith
Production Manager: Jacquie Poirier

The text of this book was composed in Belizio, Benton Sans, and Serifa.

Printed and bound in the United States
10 9 8 7 6 5 4 3 2 1

Stewart, Tabori & Chang books are available at special discounts when purchased in quantity for
premiums and promotions as well as fundraising or educational use. Special editions can also be created
to specification. For details, contact specialsales@abramsbooks.com or the address below.

THE ART OF BOOKS SINCE 1949
115 West 18th Street
New York, NY 10011
www.abramsbooks.com

CONTENTS

RIVERSIDE COLONIAL REVIVAL
CHAPTER 01 | PG 12

NEW ENGLAND FARMHOUSE
CHAPTER 02 | PG 34

DUTCH COLONIAL REVIVAL
CHAPTER 06 | PG 118

SHINGLE-STYLE VICTORIAN
CHAPTER 07 | PG 136

Introduction

O Our television camera captures thirty frames per second, and each one of those frames is like a mini-picture of the homes on which we work. Add up all of the episodes over the last ten seasons, and we end up with more than a

dozen homes—and fourteen million frames of film. So why, you may ask, would anyone publish a book with a mere 270 photographs of these same projects? Before you demand your money back, let me explain.

This Old House—the television show—is mostly about sawdust and process. We take old homes and homeowners' dreams, tear them apart, and put them back together again, relying not just on hammers and saws but on generations of know-how. It isn't until the last half of the last episode of each season that we spend any time showing off the fruits of all that labor. During those quick tours, viewers get brief glimpses of finished kitchens and family rooms before

the credits roll and another season comes to an end. Television is like that. It's powerful, but not permanent. But a book? A book is something you can reach for, come back to, or pass along.

So while the television show uses moving images to capture the lengthy process of renovating a house, this book uses still photographs to present the permanent beauty of a well-crafted home. On the following pages you will see what even the most loyal viewers of our show have never seen: ten completed *This Old House* projects in all their glory, captured in spectacular photographs, not split-second frames of film.

The pictures and stories that follow are a small contribution to a much larger effort. When you suddenly become part of a well-established organization (as I did) that is as widely respected as *This Old House,* and when you get a disproportionate amount of the attention (as I do) because you happen to talk while others work, you feel an obligation to contribute in any way you can.

So this book is also a celebration of the people who create these beautiful spaces.

Homes aren't renovated by "us" or "them." The work is done by real people who labor for long days over many months, shaping and fitting materials, transforming pallets of supplies into spaces that offer both comfort and shelter. Of course, our viewers are on a first-name basis with some of those people—Tom, Roger, Richard, and Norm. But there are many others—tradesmen, designers, artists, homeowners—who are equally dedicated to building beautiful homes and making great television. Gathering their work in a single volume is a fitting way to celebrate their efforts.

So whether you've seen fourteen or fourteen million of those frames of film, I know you will enjoy the 270 beautiful images we've settled on here. They tell the story of *This Old House* in a totally different way. Enjoy! ※

FACING PAGE: Details make the difference. A plaster bead called "cake frosting" applied with an actual pastry bag adorns the bedroom walls of this Los Angeles house.

LEFT: Renovations require imagination. An oak railing turns where stairway clearance narrows.

01. RIVERSIDE COLONIAL REVIVAL

"**Stalkers.**" That's how they described themselves—desperate, hungry house hunters who had stalked their new neighborhood for years. They coveted the neighborhood and freely admitted it. Now, if you met our homeowners, Allison and Raveen Sharma, you would never think of them as stalkers. They were polite, intelligent, and motivated—each holding down a job while raising two delightful children. The kids shared their mother's bright smile and their father's easygoing disposition, and they also shared their parents' love of this neighborhood.

BEFORE

LEFT: A poorly constructed sunporch added years after the house was built provided the only views of the river. We completely removed it and built a new one.

RIGHT: The entry hall was dark and in desperate need of an update. I was amazed to see string being used in place of proper balusters on the staircase.

So why did the Sharmas become stalkers? What was the object of their obsession? A house, of course, and more specifically, a house in a particular neighborhood of Auburndale, Massachusetts.

The first time I drove to the house in Auburndale, I myself became hungry. I wanted what I saw, which was a wide, tree-lined street with a center island covered with grass and more trees. Kids walked to the bus stop, neighbors shared friendly waves, and the houses were well kept. The things you couldn't see made the neighborhood even more desirable—a seven-mile commute to downtown Boston, great schools, and the city's famous Charles River. Behind every house, all one hundred of them tucked into this peninsula, was waterfront property! Who *wouldn't* stalk such a neighborhood?

The Sharma family had friends in this neighborhood and they wanted in. The price of admission? An outdated, uninspired box of a home loosely defined as a Colonial Revival but with a featureless façade that defied even that broad definition. It had been built in the 1940s, a custom home designed by an architect. It still had all of the original odd architectural choices, like an attached flat-roof garage that protruded far out in front of the house and a small dark entrance that receded back from the front as much as the garage projected forward. The home had been virtually untouched, architecturally speaking, for the past seventy years. It was worn, it was tired, and it shared many old-house afflictions: peeling paint, small windows, dark interiors, outdated mechanical systems, and a dearth of detail.

But the house's biggest shortcoming was its complete disregard for the river behind it. While neighbors had rolling lawns leading to small docks for kayaks and canoes, or sunrooms with sweeping, unobstructed views of the river, our house had a tiny sunroom with large and leaky windows, fake-oak paneling, and a soon-to-be-discovered nest of carpenter ants. As the ants slowly devoured the porch, only they had a decent view of the river!

And the homeowner's view? In the summertime, instead of the water, it was an unsightly mound of earth, maybe twenty-five feet high, covered with poison ivy and other tangled underbrush. It was once thought to be an Indian burial spot, a

FACING PAGE, TOP: The small galley kitchen, virtually untouched for seventy years, still had its vintage stove and double-swing door.

FACING PAGE, BOTTOM: The second floor had adjoining pink bathrooms with a shared tub. Both bathrooms were stripped back to their studs.

ABOVE LEFT: This is the old kitchen after we gutted it and removed the walls that separated it from the dining room and entry hall. The original window opening was in a perfect spot, so we kept it there.

ABOVE RIGHT: We cut through the existing foundation wall and built a small addition off the back of the house, creating a new family room downstairs and a sunroom upstairs.

AFTER

myth later debunked and replaced with a more plausible reality: The mound was a dumping area for construction fill removed to make way for the home's foundation seventy years earlier. And in the winter? Well, we heard the sunroom was so cold you were more likely to see your breath than the Charles River.

So our job was to open the house up to the water, as should have been done when it was first constructed seven decades earlier. Originally, the theory went, the home turned its back on the river because in the '40s the Charles was a dirty eyesore. And while this was partly true—for decades the river was used to transport residential and industrial waste, leaching riverside landfills polluted the water, and some sections had become a repository for old cars and appliances—the real reason was probably closer to the one offered by the home's most recent occupants.

The home's previous owner was Jules Aarons, a physicist and noted photographer, who excelled at street photography and whose work was well respected; during construction an exhibit of his work was shown at the Boston Public Library. Although Aarons passed away a year and a half before we started filming, we had the pleasure of meeting his two sons, who regaled

FACING PAGE: The new sunroom, with two walls of casement windows looking out over the Charles River. Sconces and a tray ceiling add detail to the sun-drenched space.

ABOVE LEFT: A new open floor plan and vibrant colors transform the once dark house. The dining room sits adjacent to the larger kitchen and fireplace seating area.

ABOVE RIGHT: The original staircase had a solid wall on one side that we partially removed and replaced with balusters to open up the views. We added a small powder room off the entryway.

PREVIOUS PAGE, LEFT: New wood floors, a door flanked by windows, sconces, and a coatroom make the entryway warm and welcoming for the first time in seventy years.

PREVIOUS PAGE, RIGHT: We enlarged the narrow basement to make way for a new family room. Radiant heat underneath, deep windowsills, and access to the yard and river beyond completely transformed the house.

us with stories of their childhood growing up in this home. They told us their father never had much interest in the backyard or the river beyond. Instead, when he wasn't working as a civilian scientist for the air force, Aarons spent his time walking the immigrant-filled streets of Boston's nearly forgotten West End taking pictures, or in his basement darkroom bringing those pictures to life. I saw his photography on display, and it was indeed a worthy pursuit. We were all pleased to find his stainless-steel developing sink still in the basement when the renovation began.

Tom Silva and his crew used several tricks to open the house up to the river, and the most effective was to tear down the old sunporch (before the carpenter ants did!) and rebuild it over a new addition off the back of the house. Given the slope of the property, the rear of the house enjoyed a full-height basement, which meant the new sunporch was about twelve feet off the ground, giving it a clear line of sight to the water. Tom wrapped the porch in glass on three sides and, on the south wall, installed a large sliding door that opened onto a new porch that connected the new kitchen and the backyard for the first time.

FACING PAGE: We tucked the dining room into a sunlit corner that now opens onto the main living space. Richly colored fabrics complement the bold paint color and the tones of the furniture.

ABOVE: A flat kitchen window is boxed out to create a deep sill above the "leathered" granite countertops.

CASEMENT WINDOWS

I've never been a fan of casement windows. Maybe it's because when I was growing up all I ever knew were double-hung windows. Or maybe it's because the double-hung window seems to be the most traditional choice—I am an old-house guy, after all. Whatever the cause, my opinion of casement windows changed completely during the Auburndale project, for two reasons. First, I bought a new house during this project that had a mix of double-hung and casement windows and, after I had lived there a very short time, it occurred to me that I much preferred casement windows. While double-hung windows often stick, leak at the meeting rail, and by design only open halfway at any given time, casement windows do none of that. They open easily with a smooth turn of a hand crank, they seal out air completely around the entire perimeter of the opening, and they swing out so that you can enjoy the window's entire opening.

At the same time that I was living through this compare-and-contrast scenario, the homeowners in Auburndale were struggling with what to do with their decrepit casement windows—replace them with double-hungs or stay with the home's original form and treat themselves to new, efficient units. As you can see from the adjacent pictures, they chose casement windows. It was a good choice, not just for the reasons I had discovered in my own house, but also for reasons that good architects and builders have understood for generations.

Because casement windows don't have a center meeting rail, they have a different lite pattern than double-hung windows, a pattern I believe is more symmetrical, repeatable, and pleasing. Window "lites," the individual panes of glass surrounded by "muttons," do a lot to improve our view of the world and to help us process what we see outside. It is an idea expressed perfectly by Christopher Alexander in his book *A Pattern Language.* He thinks of windows this way:

"When we consider a window as an eye through which to see a view, we must recognize that it is the extent to which the window frames the view, that increases the view, increases its intensity, increases its variety, even increases the number of views we seem to see—and it is because of this that windows which are broken into smaller windows, and windows which are filled with tiny panes, put us so intimately in touch with what is on the other side."

And when a waterfront view is on the other side and it has been ignored and obstructed for seventy years, how it is enjoyed is critical. The choice of casement windows in this house was the perfect way to frame, to increase, and to intensify the view of the water that first captivated our homeowners. ✕

PREVIOUS PAGE LEFT: From the kitchen, you can now see all the way through the house, and enjoy the light and views from the sunporch throughout the entire first floor.

TOP: We replaced dark paneling in the old living room with lively colors and crisp millwork.

BOTTOM: Two doorways provide easy access to the new kitchen from both sides, helping to control traffic between the cooking and seating areas.

ABOVE: After seventy years, the vintage stove finally met its match. The recessed niche pops with more green tiles.

RIGHT: The kitchen island's freestanding legs make it feel like a piece of furniture; its bold green color is complemented by the subtle strip of tile in the white backsplash.

The effect was stunning. Light streamed deep into the house and the river seemed as if it had always been an integral part of the property instead of a forgotten feature. The casement windows and their uninterrupted patterns of "muttons" divided the light into digestible bites that danced on the floor and reflected off the plaster surfaces of the new tray ceiling. From most rooms on the first floor you could now see the river, and from *every* room you could feel the draw of the light energizing the house. And the sunporch was just the beginning.

We added four new doors to the outside, which meant there were four new ways to experience the property and the neighborhood that until now had been inaccessible. Two of those new entrances were in the basement. It had started off as a dark and narrow space but became a proper family room, complete with French doors and two walls of corner windows with deep sills clad in elegant millwork that belied the mass of the concrete foundation underneath. Insulated concrete forms (ICFs) were used to extend the house's foundation back about sixteen feet. ICFs are an ingenious replacement for the temporary wooden forms that typically hold wet concrete in place as it hardens. These clever forms snap together like Legos and are insulated on both sides, providing strength, simplicity, and insulation, all in one package.

LEFT: The home now has a proper coat-room, bringing some order to the busy household of four.

RIGHT: Despite the open floor plan, sun-drenched corners with their own views create separate and private spaces.

But it was the kitchen, as it usually is, that underwent the largest transformation. Both Raveen and Allison enjoy cooking, so their obsession with a new kitchen was not surprising. The tiny galley work space, with its original painted pine cabinets, seventy-year-old stove, and chipped laminate countertops, may have added to their fixation. So Tommy and his crew set upon the dated space with ferocity. They stripped it bare, removed a partition wall, inserted a steel beam, abated all sorts of nastiness like lead and asbestos, enlarged and added windows, and added two interior doorways as well as an exterior door. And while doing all this, Tommy also navigated the inevitable indecision all our homeowners experience when faced with the hundreds of choices that a new kitchen requires. At one point the new island was slated to have a stove top in its center, then a large sink, then no sink, before Raveen and Allison finally settled instead on a small prep sink in the corner.

A six-burner stove, sufficient cabinet space, and stone countertops would satisfy most homeowners' dreams. But shiny new appliances and updated lighting don't guarantee you'll get a kitchen right. In our kitchen, getting it right was the result of the usual factors—a well-thought-through plan that allows two people to work on top of each other without complaint—but also other ingredients, like a simple glass-tile detail coursing through the backsplash or the texture of the granite countertops. Called

"leathered" or "antiqued," the smooth surface of the granite is burnished with wired brushes until the shine and evenness are gone, leaving behind small indentations that give the stone some age without the wear. The effect was the ideal balance between old and new, and in many ways the leathered granite was the perfect example of how Raveen and Allison got their kitchen, and all its details, just right.

When a single bathroom is shared by two adjoining bedrooms, it's often called a Jack and Jill bathroom. But when a single bedroom is adjoined by *two bathrooms*, it's called odd. And when those two bathrooms are covered in Pepto Bismol–pink tiles, well, I'm not sure what you call it, but that was the defining feature of the second floor, and anyone who walked through this peculiar space knew changes were in order. So both bathrooms were gutted down to the studs, the plumbing was reconfigured, and the two spaces were entirely rebuilt as two separate rooms. The kids shared one of the bathrooms. It was modest in size but lavishly wrapped in traditional white subway tile with black accents and fresh new fixtures, and a new window that let in lots of natural light. Allison and Raveen had the second bathroom all to themselves.

It's a paradox to me how tile, so hard and cold in your hand, can add such richness and pleasing texture to a bathroom when it adorns the walls and floor, but it can. And it did in the master bathroom. We installed tile on every inch of the floor and on every inch

ABOVE: A new addition, with plenty of windows and light, transforms the basement into a spacious family room. The designer's trick: "Don't treat it like a basement, and it won't feel like one."

TOP LEFT AND RIGHT: The master bedroom remained the same size but has new windows, a deck, and spalike colors and fabrics that create a serene space.

FACING PAGE: One of my favorite features is this mirrored wall, interrupted by the new window. Cool colors and materials complete the master bath.

of the shower stall. We laid small one-inch squares with rough edges in a symmetrical grid underfoot, bordered by more of the same. We laid marble tiles in a brick pattern in the shower, and the four-by-eight-inch rectangles were ingeniously cut from eight-by-eight-inch square tiles to save money. They matched the marble countertop and marble baseboard. But my favorite feature of the entire room was a full-wall mirror above the vanity and its two sinks, punctuated with a window placed right in the center of this now shimmering, reflective wall. Few contractors other than Tom Silva would have even entertained the complexity of trimming and fitting glass, wood, and plaster in this way.

In the end, Allison and Raveen were right to covet the odd box of a house on the river because when we were done with it they had themselves a beautiful new house, in a great neighborhood, that made the most of the Charles River behind it. And as I drove away from the project house for the last time, I added the Sharma house to the list of things I loved about this little corner of Auburndale, Massachusetts.

Close Up
Richard Trethewey

During the first season of *This Old House* back in 1979, the show hired Richard Trethewey's father, Ron, as the plumber for the project and put him on camera to explain the intricacies of his trade. But Ron was nervous about talking to the camera, and in his desperation to step out of the spotlight he offered up his son instead, joking that Richard was "too dumb to be nervous." A great line, but entirely without merit.

Richard is a smart guy—a very smart guy. He understands the science of plumbing, heating, and cooling better than anyone I know. He regularly travels around the world in search of the latest technologies to make our buildings comfortable, and he works in a complicated industry. It's full of aphorisms like "heat goes to cold" and "more goes to less," but the jargon belies the very complex laws of thermodynamics a plumber must master.

I remember filming with Richard one day in the *Ask This Old House* loft, knocking off scenes about low water pressure and on-demand water heaters. I was firing questions and Richard was firing back. "Does a house farther away from a water tower have lower water pressure?" I asked. "Sure, pressure depends on friction and weight, or the distance and elevation of the tower," he responded, before rattling off the relevant formula. Discussing the water heater, I wondered, "Does it matter if I use propane or natural gas?" Of course it matters, he told me, then rattled off the number of BTUs in a therm of each fuel, and even calculated their respective costs.

It was amazing. It was impossible to stump the guy. But most impressive was the fact that Richard not only knew the answers, he also knew how to explain them, in simple terms that were precise and understandable in equal measure. And he's still doing it thirty years later, proof that, all jokes aside, his dad had it right—he was the perfect man for the job.

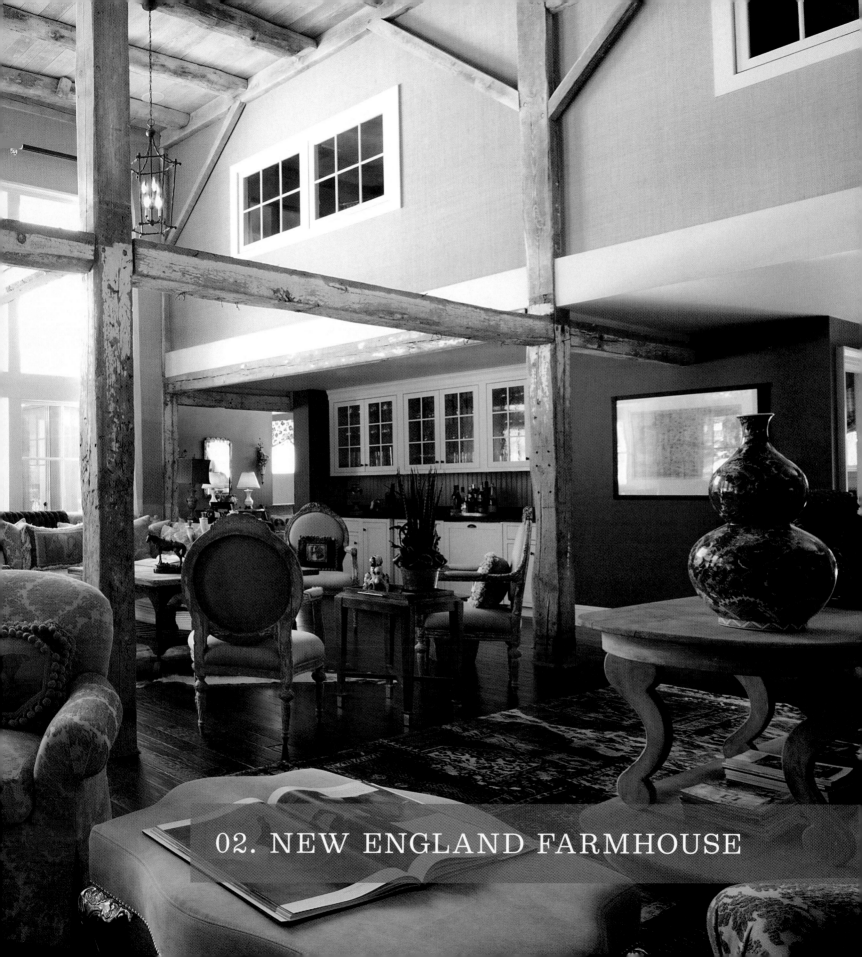

02. NEW ENGLAND FARMHOUSE

People ask me all the time to reveal my favorite *This Old House* project, so I'll just come right out with it: it's the Carlisle barn that we renovated in 2004. We planned this massive undertaking as a celebration of the show's twenty-fifth anniversary, so we decided to do something different—something extravagant. Our typical television season follows a familiar formula: We make sixteen episodes working with homeowners somewhere in or around Boston, our home base, and then ten episodes working with homeowners in a warm-weather climate like Austin or Los Angeles. For the Carlisle project, we decided to go another route. First, we bought the property outright so our team could do essentially whatever we pleased.

LEFT: One-third of the original homestead was a working barn, home to hundreds of chickens just months before we purchased the property. Eventually, this building was transformed into a grand living hall.

FACING PAGE: We dismantled the structure under the barn because it was beyond repair. To prepare for the work, we had to jack up the building nearly two feet and temporarily hold it in place with cribbing and steel "pins," seen here. The ell connecting the main house to the barn had a different fate. It was demolished by an excavator and completely rebuilt (lower left).

ABOVE AND FACING PAGE: Poorly constructed and designed, the ell that ran between the main house and the barn came down easily. We pulverized it into its own basement. Once the debris was hauled away, we patched the two adjoining buildings and began work on a new ell.

This meant budget flexibility and lots of big thinking from a talented team of builders. Second, we dedicated all twenty-six of the season's episodes to this single project so we could dive deeper into the story of the house and show an abundance of techniques and materials that could never fit into a conventional renovation. The sky was the limit. Finally, when the renovation was complete, we invited some of the top interior designers in the country to outfit the house for a public viewing that would last a month and attract thousands of visitors.

The house comprised three distinct buildings built at different times for different purposes. It's a classic New England farmhouse story: The family starts with a modest home—in this case, a small Greek Revival house that was a room and a half wide and two rooms deep. Then, they add a barn a little ways from

the house to shelter livestock and farming equipment. As the family grows over the years, the house grows with them, gaining more living space and perhaps an addition to connect the house to the barn. And that was exactly the case with our property, where a low-slung, one-story ell, housing the kitchen and dining room, connected the main house and the barn. These three buildings—the Greek Revival, the ell, and the barn—offered a perfect mix of styles, allowing us to demonstrate three distinct methods of construction. We'd *renovate* the Greek Revival, *reconstruct* the ell, and *repurpose* the barn.

Work began with the ell. This poorly designed and constructed building wasn't worth saving, so Tom Silva cut it away from the main house on one side and from the barn on the other using nothing more than a reciprocating saw.

40 AFTER

Then it only took about an hour for a large excavator to demolish the rest of the structure and pulverize everything, pushing it into the dilapidated basement. Roof, walls, windows, doors, and kitchen cabinets were shattered into little bits, making for a terrific spectacle that mesmerized the cast, crew, and dozens of onlookers who had stopped to see the action.

Reconstruction of the ell began as soon as the debris was hauled away. Well, technically, reconstruction began *before* the old building was torn down, since we prefabricated the new foundation and the shell of the house off-site. We used precast concrete panels with rigid insulation and framing studs already attached for the foundation. Tommy and his crew had prepared a stone base onto which a crane hauled the tall panels, and then the dozens of panels were glued and bolted together. It only took a day or two to assemble the foundation and another day to fuss with it and marry it to the rubble-stone foundations under the main house and the barn.

We then set large prefabricated wall panels on top of the foundation. These structurally insulated panels (SIPs) were also prefabricated off-site and went into place almost as quickly as the foundation. SIPs, which provide a near-continuous layer of insulation sandwiched between layers of plywoodlike material, require

FACING PAGE: The centerpiece of the old barn, now the "living hall," is a massive fireplace. The wood floor was delicately scribed around the fieldstone hearth. A granite mantel and stucco flue complement the original barn boards and beams.

ABOVE LEFT: High windows that limit views of the busy road flank the new back door, and slate underfoot will handle the heavy traffic in this busy entryway.

ABOVE RIGHT: Tall windows in the living hall are dressed with custom drapes; the colors echo the grass and sky seen through the windows.

PREVIOUS PAGE, LEFT: A work station adjacent to the kitchen sits in the center of a long hallway running the length of the new ell, so parents can easily supervise the kids' homework. More high windows provide light and privacy.

PREVIOUS PAGE, RIGHT: The dining room, adjacent to the work station, is covered with a sumptuous red silk fabric divided with thin battens. Designer Alexa Hampton chose every detail from the moulding profile to the switchplate covers on the wall.

ABOVE: An addition off the back of the house made room for a new first-floor master suite. In the bathroom, the soft green paint plays off the stone tub surround; the raised window provides privacy and lots of light that casts shadows on the irregular handmade tiles wrapping around the bathing area.

RIGHT: In the bedroom, asymmetrical roof lines and corner windows distinguish this space from the original Greek Revival house. Twelve-inch-square, luminescent paper tiles cover the walls.

fewer structural studs and produce fewer air gaps. That means less heat loss in the winter and a more comfortable and energy-efficient house year-round.

Inside the newly constructed ell went a new kitchen, dining room, office space, and access to a new parking deck out front. While modern modular materials served as the underpinning, the exterior was clad in the traditional look of clapboards and a copper roof. The new windows on the front of the ell were small and placed high enough to limit the views of the busy street, while the glass on the back was abundant, running from floor to ceiling in some places. Several doors opened onto a new stone patio and landscaped yard. And the ell was reconnected to the Greek Revival on one end and the barn on the other—but not before those two spaces also received the *This Old House* treatment.

Repurposing the barn was by far the most challenging part of the project. Just a few months before we purchased the property, it had been home to hundreds of chickens, and before they moved in, cows, goats, and horses had called the barn home. Animals had occupied this barn for decades and had left behind quite a mess, requiring yeoman's work to make the space suitable for people. The first floor of the barn and much of the structure beneath it had rotted beyond repair, so the entire building—several hundred tons of it—had to be jacked up about two feet so Tommy could install new posts, beams, and floors. It was a bear of a task. In most cases we try not to let our cameras disrupt the work, but it's not often that we get to jack a building right off of its foundation, so we wanted to make sure we captured the event for the show. Since we film with only one camera and wanted to catch the action from several angles, we had to lift the barn up and down *repeatedly*. It was a first for Eddie Couturier, our patient building-mover, and it went on for so long that I remember leaving the job site for a fresh cup of coffee, only to find the big old barn still dancing up and down for the camera when I returned an hour later.

The architect redesigned the barn into what he called the "living hall," a grand space where family and friends could gather. Two guest bedrooms would now occupy part of the second floor, while the haylofts and the remaining upper floor were removed to make way for a vaulted two-story great room with a massive fireplace and exposed chimney in its center. The northeast side of the room now features a wall of floor-to-ceiling windows, while off the back is a new screened porch; a wet bar is adjacent to the foyer and kitchen. In the southwest corner there is a one-story alcove for reading or watching television; the low ceiling and intimate proportions of this space make it snug and cozy despite its location next to the cavernous great room.

We preserved many of the barn's original materials and left them exposed to serve as a reminder of the building's original use. The posts, beams, half-sawed

LEFT: The original Greek Revival now has a bathroom and two bedrooms upstairs; the designers made sure these two spaces were unique by choosing contrasting bright pink and cool blue colors.

RIGHT: A corner window in the bedroom gives views of the side yard.

logs used for floor joists, and rough boards that made up the ceilings went virtually untouched, getting nothing more than a soft whitewash finish. Nails, pegs, and decades' worth of blemishes remained—only the plaster walls, now covered in grass-cloth wallpaper, and the new hickory floor made it clear that the chickens no longer ruled this roost.

Finally, we moved to the original Greek Revival. Like the barn, much of this building's first floor was rotted and required major reconstruction and foundation work. But unlike the other two buildings, the main house was well designed: It had good symmetry and well-balanced proportions, features common to a Greek Revival. We left those proportions untouched even as we changed the building's use considerably. We removed the front staircase just off the original living room and transformed that space into a tranquil library. A laundry room, a half-bath, and a new first-floor master suite were built in the space of the existing house and a new addition off the back. Upstairs, we raised ceilings and moved walls to create two bedrooms and a bathroom. The whole building was connected to the newly rebuilt ell by an elegant hallway, with two steps to announce the transition between old and new.

The construction and renovation physically tied the three buildings together, but they were still three distinct spaces in need of cohesion and connectedness.

FACING PAGE, TOP LEFT: Public and private parts of the house are separated by two narrow doors and a hallway, where a dark ceiling, shuttered windows, and textured fabric–covered walls create a sense of compression that is released upon entering the vaulted dining room.

FACING PAGE, RIGHT: In the master bathroom the floor tiles match the stone counters of the double vanity and a small television is hidden behind a two-way mirror on the right medicine cabinet.

FACING PAGE, BOTTOM: Freestanding cabinets with glass doors show off the family's collection of books and art in the library.

LEFT: We preserved the wood timbers of the original barn and left them exposed throughout the new living hall. We covered most of the barn-board sheathing with plaster and then applied a variety of finishes, such as the combed red paint shown here.

BOTTOM LEFT: A long hallway in the ell connects all of its rooms and provides vistas through the house; even first-time visitors can easily navigate their way around.

BOTTOM RIGHT: Shutters over the high windows in the hallway provide added privacy and even change the mood as you move from the public to the private areas of the house.

That was the job of the designers—all nine of them. From the grand living hall in the barn to the sumptuous dining room in the ell, all the way to the utilitarian laundry room in the main house, some of the finest minds in the field of design filled the house with unique styles. The dining-room walls were covered in silk fabric, while one bathroom's walls were covered in felt. The master bedroom was papered in twelve-inch turquoise squares, while an adjoining hallway was painted in another twelve-inch checkerboard design that played off the nearby paper. Each room, and even different corners of the same room, became layered and textured expressions of the individual designers decorating them. But despite all the different hands at work, the final effect was surprisingly seamless. Walking the length of the house from the grand living hall in the old barn to the library at the opposite end, we could feel that the entire space was complete and connected. And while I suspect this was the feeling of the thousands of visitors who took advantage of our month-long open house, I *know* it was the feeling of the home's new owners.

BOTTOM LEFT: In the old barn, half of the new living hall is wide open, with two-story, floor-to-ceiling windows and exposed beams. The walls are covered in an earthy grass cloth and the wet bar at the end of the room was purposely placed near the kitchen.

BOTTOM RIGHT: The dining room represents the end of the public space; the library and bedrooms lie beyond the narrow hallway. Two short steps mark the entryway into the original Greek Revival.

FACING PAGE: We deliberately left the façade of the old barn intact, giving no hint of the grand living hall that it now housed. The original barn door opens onto a barn court, a space that transitions between inside and out, old and new.

Several months after filming was complete, we sold the house to a family of four who had first seen it during the public tours. When I visited with them five years later, I was thrilled and a bit surprised to find the house in nearly the exact condition in which we left it. Every piece of wallpaper, every paint color was the same, and the family was using the house exactly as we had imagined. Even its furnishings were similar to the ones used by the designers. This was a testament to the collective wisdom and decades of experience of the architect, the designers, and the *This Old House* team. To me, the Carlisle barn was the grandest and most thoughtful space we ever worked on, and it was a joy to be back in this sprawling home—a celebration of twenty-five years of hard work and skillful renovations.

FACING PAGE: We added a sealed gas fireplace to the library and were careful to repeat the symmetry found elsewhere in the original Greek Revival. White-on-white walls add to the serenity of the room.

ABOVE: A low ceiling in one half of the living hall creates an intimate nook for reading or watching television. We covered the old barn walls with plaster but whitewashed the beams and planks that make up the ceiling and left them exposed.

Close Up
Tom Silva

Tom Silva sees the world differently than most people. I didn't fully understand this until years after we first met. In 2002, I wrote to *Ask This Old House* about problems with *my* old house. That e-mail and a producer brought Tommy to my home, and with the camera rolling, he patiently helped me replace an old-fashioned corner bead. My wife and I were in the midst of renovating and were happy for the help. But before Tommy left my house that day, he secretly screwed and glued my tools to my kitchen floor! Who does that? To a complete stranger!

Tommy does; he likes to joke around. But his prankster ways belie a deeper thoughtfulness. Just when you're convinced he's concocting a way to let all the air out of your tires, you realize he's actually figuring out how to restructure a hundred-year-old floor. As he scratches his ideas on a napkin, you begin to recognize that he is truly an artist.

After unscrewing the tools from my kitchen floor that day in 2002, I continued my renovation, gutting most of the rooms in the house and putting them back together one stud at a time. It took me months to do what a professional could do in days, but when I was done I experienced an amazing feeling—I could see through the walls. Hanging pictures on freshly painted plaster was easy—I remembered where I placed every stud. And that's when it dawned on me. Tom Silva sees through walls every day. He's worked on so many houses and so thoroughly understands how they are built that he can walk into a house for the first time and know exactly what's behind the walls. He fixes them in his mind before he ever swings a hammer. So if Tom ever comes to your house, be grateful . . . but be careful.

03. SECOND EMPIRE VICTORIAN

W

e see a lot of old, run-down houses; in fact, they are our stock-in-trade. And no matter how bad the disrepair, just about any house has some redeeming value. Maybe it's in a great neighborhood, maybe the bones of the house are sturdy and it only needs a cosmetic facelift, maybe the interior details are rich and abundant, or maybe with the hardest cases we don't care so much for the house but love the homeowners. The house we chose in Roxbury, Massachusetts, had none of these qualities.

BEFORE

LEFT: Most people would not have saved this building, and by the time we stripped off four layers of siding and got down to the exterior sheathing shown here, even we were wondering if the building was worth preserving.

FACING PAGE: The house had been abandoned for at least a year by the time we got involved. Weather and neglect had taken their toll: We couldn't even walk in one of the kitchens (shown here) without risk of falling through the floor.

Our house was abandoned and boarded up. A hole in the roof let in rainwater that had created a hole in the second floor that had created another hole in the first floor. The kitchen floor had completely collapsed; we couldn't even walk on it without risk of falling through the framing. The plaster was ruined, the floors that hadn't collapsed yet were beyond salvage, and most of the original details like the plaster medallions and the marble mantelpieces had either deteriorated or been stolen. And in a telling moment, Norm Abram, who has been part of every *This Old House* project since our beginning in 1979, proclaimed the Roxbury house one of the most decrepit homes we'd ever worked on. And to top it all off, there was no hope of a delightful homeowner who could help us get past all of these troubles—the house was in foreclosure and owned by the bank.

So why dive into such a losing proposition? Partly for nostalgia's sake, but mostly to give something back to the city where it all began. In 2009, *This Old House* celebrated its thirtieth anniversary, and in honor of that proud event the team decided we should return to our roots. The first house *This Old House* ever worked on was in Dorchester, a neighborhood of Boston less than a mile and a half from our current house in Roxbury (another Boston neighborhood), and the cast and crew liked the idea of returning to the place where it all started.

The national housing crisis also reached its peak in 2009. The collapse of the financial markets led to the collapse of the real-estate market, which in many ways is leading to the collapse of neighborhoods all across the country. Roxbury is one of those neighborhoods. Over a two-year period, more than one thousand homes went into foreclosure in Boston, and the city's mayor had declared the section of Roxbury where our house stood—barely—as the ground zero of foreclosures. For us that sealed the deal.

This Old House partnered with Boston mayor Tom Menino and with Nuestra Comunidad, a local nonprofit whose mission was to fix up and build affordable housing for the people of Boston and, in particular, for the people of Roxbury. Together we would refurbish the house, hopefully for a modest sum, and then sell it to a deserving homeowner for a below-market rate. In the process we'd save an old home, help a resident of the city, and hopefully revitalize a proud old neighborhood. These were all worthy goals that would mean *lots* of work.

FACING PAGE: Despite its state of disrepair, the house had original details that were worth saving, like the marble fireplace surround in the living room and the bay windows at the front of the house. But you had to look hard to find them in all the mess.

ABOVE LEFT: The two-family house was divided down the center; originally we tried to save both staircases and their balustrades, but in the end they too were swept away in the demolition.

ABOVE RIGHT: Someone had built an addition onto the back of the house years after it was originally constructed. We stripped it off and poured a new foundation in preparation for a two-story addition for new family rooms and bedrooms.

AFTER

Our house was built in the 1870s in the Second Empire style, with its distinctive mansard roof. In 2009 it was a two-family home, and a firewall that ran through the center of the house, uncovered during the renovation, suggested it had been built that way originally. Each unit of the house went front to back and up two stories, and in later years an addition was built off the back of the house. There were two front doors, separate but nearly symmetrical, and on one side of the house there was a two-story bay with three windows punched through it on each floor. This feature added a bit of grandeur to the house but also a bit of mystery. It appeared original to the building, although we couldn't say for sure, and no one could figure out why a similar bay hadn't been built on the other side.

The scope and specifics of our work were dictated by two separate but equally important factors. First, with no homeowner at the outset, we had to renovate the house so that it could serve a range of people—from a family of four to a single person with a roommate. We also knew that the house would eventually become the property of someone who met Nuestra Comunidad's income criteria, which meant the cost of owning and operating the house could not be an undue burden.

FACING PAGE: The front of the house is formal, with dark wood floors and large moulding reminiscent of the home's original features. Eleven-foot-high ceilings show off the grandeur of the structure.

TOP LEFT: We used bright colors and details like the corbels under the mansard roof to return some Victorian flourish to the exterior. New clapboard and shingles are a vast improvement over the many layers we stripped off the house.

TOP RIGHT: A new eating area is part of the addition to the back of the house. The dark paint color adds a formality to this space and sets it off from the adjacent kitchen and family room.

ABOVE LEFT: Marble is a traditional choice for fireplace mantels in Boston and elsewhere, and we used it here to add some formality to the parlor. The white marble sets off the black cast-iron door.

ABOVE RIGHT: This home's plaster ceiling medallion happened to be a near-perfect match for a medallion we had restored during another Boston project nine years earlier, so we used the same mold to replicate it here.

FACING PAGE: Despite our best intentions, the original staircase and balustrade couldn't be saved, so we rebuilt them. The home's original newel post now lives in the *Ask This Old House* loft, among dozens of other artifacts from the two shows.

And while we always build with energy efficiency and low maintenance in mind, this time around hitting these marks was crucial.

The first order of business was tearing off the back of the house, which wasn't difficult. Even though it was probably forty to sixty years newer than the original front of the house, it too was falling apart. It did require a large piece of equipment, though, and it was strangely satisfying to strip away the piece of the house that was not original, as if it were a foreign appendage and less worthy. For some reason, when it comes to houses, new rot is more vile than old rot.

After the back was removed the roof came off, then not one, not two, but *three* layers of siding were stripped off the building. Next, part of the puddingstone foundation was removed, followed by interior plaster and then the wood flooring. Partition walls disappeared and two staircases slated for salvage evaporated when

ROXBURY PUDDINGSTONE

The choice of our Roxbury project was a deliberate attempt to connect with our first project in Dorchester, completed thirty years before. It was a fitting way to celebrate the show's thirtieth anniversary, and fortunately the connections were plentiful. Both houses were in Boston neighborhoods, neither house had a homeowner when construction started, and each home was, to be honest, a bit of a sad case. But the strongest connection between the two homes may have been the very ground upon which they were built.

Much of the bedrock beneath Boston and the surrounding towns is a conglomerate known as Roxbury puddingstone. It's a sedimentary mix with a distinctive look marked by smooth, round stones suspended in brown sediment. There is some mystery as to how it came to be, but the best theory, and the most widely held, is that it was formed by fast-moving water carrying rocks and mud, until the mix was deposited and then turned to stone.

Roxbury puddingstone was widely used in Boston in the 1800s and early 1900s to build churches, the spans of stone dams, and the foundations of many homes. In 1830 Oliver Wendell Holmes even penned a charming ode to this inert conglomeration. Titled "The Dorcester Giant," it tells the story of a giant who locks up his children and his scold of a wife. To keep them happy during their confinement he feeds them pudding. Alas, his scheme doesn't work and things get messy when the angry children and wife protest by hurling their pudding hither and yon:

They flung it over Roxbury hills,
They flung it over the plain,
And all over Milton and Dorcester too
Great lumps of pudding the giants threw;
They tumbled thick as rain.

From its spot halfway up a hill near Coppens Square, the Dorchester house has distant views of downtown Boston to the north and the Atlantic Ocean to the east. But to the west, the view is dominated by St. Peter's Church, a nineteenth-century landmark whose structure was built of Roxbury puddingstone excavated from its site. The same mix was used to build the foundation of our house in Roxbury, and although it was a major challenge for builder David Lopes, who had to replace part of it with today's preferred conglomerate, concrete, much of the puddingstone foundation still sits there under the house, in a state of permanent suspension. ⋈

the film crew was off-site. I returned to the house one day to find nothing but a sorry-looking wooden box, with only the mansard roof profile to suggest the structure was ever a home, rather than some century-old warehouse misplaced in a residential neighborhood. It was then that most of us realized that if the triumvirate of *This Old House*, Nuestra Comunidad, and the mayor's office had not been involved, this house would have been scraped off the property and forgotten forever.

But we *were* involved and the house would stay, so we began piecing it back together. We decided three bedrooms and a full bath on the second floor was the right mix for our yet-to-be-determined homeowner. Downstairs, the team built a small kitchen with a separate eating space, and the two were adjacent to the new family room that was placed in a small one-story addition off the recently demolished rear of the house.

The character of the new space is, in a word, elegant. First-floor ceilings are nearly eleven feet high, the mill work is sophisticated and equally impressive, the colors are mostly soft tones of white and beige, and the kitchen cabinets travel all the way up those eleven-foot walls to the ceiling, just as they would have in a

PREVIOUS PAGE: Only one side of the two-family house had this window bay, an oddity that none of us could explain. But one is better than none, so we meticulously restored the bay, and it became the center-piece of the first-floor parlor and second-floor bedroom.

FACING PAGE: The front doors were padlocked when we first arrived, but on the day of our wrap party, more than a hundred people—family, friends, and even the mayor of Boston—happily walked through them to join the celebration.

ABOVE: We painted the new living room in the back of the house with neutral colors and decorated it simply. A wash of sunlight and eleven-foot-high ceilings add all the necessary interest to this room.

RIGHT: We made the small kitchen look bigger by using white-on-white-on-white, for the cabinets, counters, and walls. The cabinets run all the way up the eleven-foot walls, giving the room the feeling of a traditional Victorian pantry.

proper pantry in a well-to-do Victorian home. But it is the front parlor that sets the tone for the house. On one side there is our bay, newly restored with painted wood panels, detailed casings, and light streaming through three windows. On the other side of the room is a salvaged marble mantel, reminiscent of the one that had been stolen from our house and the one that had been left to crack and deteriorate in the basement. A local architectural salvage shop that believed in our mission donated the piece, and the black veins running through the gray-and-white marble complement the freshly painted black cast-iron door that secures the firebox.

The parlor is now a sort of time machine. On one hand it transports you back 130 years to the time our house was originally conceived and constructed, and on the other hand it forces you to remember how dilapidated and close to demolition

ABOVE: Simple décor and subtle tones make the master bedroom a peaceful retreat. The crisp, clean feeling of the room is a far cry from its original state.

this elegant room had been just a mere nine months earlier. I'm not sure which bit of time travel was the longer journey.

Our house did get a homeowner eventually, a young, single woman named Lanita Tolentino. She grew up just a few blocks from our house and had recently moved back to the neighborhood to be closer to family. Toward the end of the project, she was helping with decisions, making the house her own. Not long after construction was completed and filming had wrapped, Lanita took possession of the new house on a happy day in March.

Sadly, the housing crisis has not abated, and despite our best hopes and efforts, foreclosures in Boston and Roxbury continue. But, happily, after thirty years we at *This Old House* were able to return to our roots and do what we do best: give new life to an old house and offer a deserving owner a new home.

LEFT: Originally, the home had two marble fireplace surrounds. One had been stolen at some point; the other we removed and stored in the basement until it accidentally broke during demolition. Fortunately, a local architectural salvage yard donated a close match that became a highlight of the front parlor.

BELOW: The balustrade railing turns where the staircase narrows, a graceful new detail added by our lead carpenter.

Close Up

Russ Morash

Russ has been a good friend to me—sort of. He stopped by my house while I was renovating and quickly pointed out that my amateurish ways were, well, ruining the place. He handed me a redesigned floor plan drawn on a napkin, then left. I showed up for filming once with a fresh haircut; he said I looked like an idiot. Over the years he has told me my tools are for weenies and not real carpenters, said that press interviews I've done show me in a poor light, warned me away from shilling for products, lamented my lack of training— and screamed at me on plenty of occasions.

But Russ is retired now, and I miss him—sort of. I still visit him at his house despite his old critiques and his fresh warnings to "wear Kevlar" when I come. We sit and have coffee and he berates me. Why do I go? Because, beyond a shadow of a doubt, Russ knows what he's talking about. His legacy is long and widely recognized. He is considered "the father of how-to television" for his work in launching such shows as *The French Chef*, *This Old House*, *Ask This Old House*, *The New Yankee Workshop*, and *The Victory Garden*. (He has other accomplishments, too, but if I list them all here, what will we talk about over our next coffee?)

Mostly I go to learn from a man I respect immensely. Russ may be retired but he is still our standard-bearer and continues to demand a great deal from the people who work on the programs he created. He observes and evaluates and delivers his opinions with unfiltered candor, and I am glad to hear them. So, I'll continue to go see Russ and take my beatings. And I'm happy to do it—sort of.

04. BROOKLYN BROWNSTONE

On a mild summer evening in August 2008, Kevin Costello and his wife, Karen Shen, walked with their three young sons on the wide sidewalks of Brooklyn's Prospect Heights, passing neighbors and friends out enjoying the summer evening. As they finished their stroll, they sat on the stoop of an old, run-down brownstone, watching the neighborhood pass by and smiling as they considered their good luck at having found and purchased the century-old boardinghouse behind them. In Brooklyn, stoops serve as front yards, and now this stoop in this up-and-coming neighborhood was theirs, with all of its problems—and all of its promise.

BEFORE

LEFT: The old rooming house was in desperate need of repair; the homeowner had started remodeling this bathroom before he called us in to help.

RIGHT: The building had been converted into a rooming house in the 1940s and divided into small, chopped-up spaces. Our first order of business was to reconnect these rooms and give the house better flow. Here, the first-floor front parlor is no longer a separate apartment but will soon connect to a future library and kitchen.

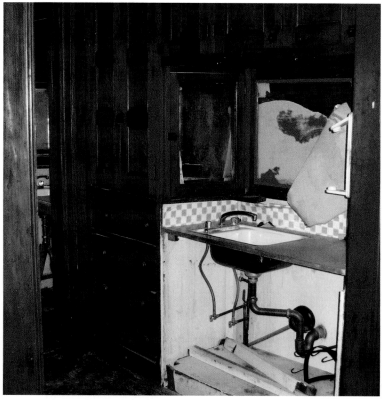

TOP LEFT: A shared staircase ran up the left side of the building, connecting the nine units of the old rooming house. The newly renovated building has three separate units, so the staircase is still public space.

TOP RIGHT: Despite previous renovations, the home still had many original details, like this woman's vanity in a bedroom closet built with bird's-eye maple. The laminate counter and sink were added when the building was converted to a rooming house.

Constructed in 1904, this brownstone was one of thousands built at the beginning of the twentieth century to provide housing for the legions of people working in the boroughs of New York City, Manhattan in particular. The exterior was now more red than brown, thanks to the latest of countless coats of paint, but it had the distinctive window bays and details befitting a home designed by the noted architect Axel Hedman. The first floor sat about eight feet above the street, with a front staircase that led both up to the elegant front door and down to the garden-level entryway. That garden, or what was left of it, was behind the house and walled in by brownstones on both sides, making it accessible only through the house. Not that anyone would *want* to access it. When *This Old House* began the Brooklyn project, the garden was completely overgrown, with loose concrete underfoot and a rusty steel arbor overhead. But as bad as the garden looked, it was in better condition than the inside of the house.

At some point, probably in the 1940s, a previous owner had converted the building into a rooming house, surely to make some money off the young men returning to New York after World War II. The building had been divided into nine separate units, and through the entryway, past the nine doorbells, a dark, narrow

LEFT: A small room at the back of the first floor was at one time its own apartment, with too many doors and too little space. When we were finished, this room became the new kitchen in the owner's unit.

BELOW: There were nearly a dozen doors off the three flights of stairs, including one that still had a manager's sign.

staircase led to nine apartment doors. When we arrived, one still had a sign that said MANAGER'S stuck to it.

Behind just about every door was a tiny apartment; most of them had sinks and cook tops squeezed into unlikely corners amid cramped living spaces. There were windows only on the front and back façades of the house, and since each floor was split into multiple apartments, most of the units had only a single source of light. The resulting darkness made small spaces seem even smaller and cast a pall over the entire house, but at least the shadows and dark corners hid most of the dirt.

Ironically, the building's neglect turned out to be its saving grace. Previous owners had made few improvements but also few changes, and that meant many of the home's original details remained intact, albeit in a strange alliance with its boardinghouse history. On the second floor, for example, a grand dressing room with built-in cabinets and closets made of bird's-eye maple remained completely intact—except for the kitchen sink awkwardly placed in the countertop of a woman's vanity, its peeling laminate an odd complement to the faded ripples of the maple.

On the main floor, wide plaster cove mouldings graced tall ceilings and oak wainscoting adorned the shabby walls. A large piece of fretwork that ran wall-to-wall

AFTER

and floor-to-ceiling separated the original front parlor, which had been converted into a separate apartment, from the original kitchen (now a second unit). The fretwork's turned spindles and fluted columns had been retrofitted to receive an old gas line for a wall-mounted sconce, but other than that modification and its worn finish, the piece was in nearly original condition. All of these details—the bird's-eye maple, the oak wainscoting, the plaster coves, the ornate fretwork— were tired and worn but they were still in the house! And after one hundred and four years and who knows how many different renovations and reconfigurations, the preservation of all these details was extraordinary. The details were, in fact, the reason Karen and Kevin fell in love with the building, and as they sat on their stoop that summer evening, aware of the work that lay ahead of them, they were eager to get started.

And so were we. *This Old House* had never worked in New York City before, and now that we were there, it made sense to work on the city's iconic housing style: the brownstone. To me, the word "brownstone" inspires visions of elegant façades and stately buildings lining the avenues of expensive neighborhoods in New York, Boston, or other American cities. But the truth about these buildings is that in many neighborhoods, they were designed for middle-income families: worker housing, rolled out four to six at a time by developers building densely packed, affordable homes in much the same way that modern subdivisions are built today. There's a

FACING PAGE: The foyer retained all of its original woodwork, including arches, fluted columns, turned spindles, and raised-panel wainscoting. Every inch was painstakingly restored by hand.

ABOVE: The woodwork restoration stands up to close inspection.

THIS PAGE: We restored a fireplace and the window-bay woodwork in the master bedroom on the second floor. Adding a picture rail and a second paint color is a good way to break up the scale of a large wall.

FACING PAGE: Details abound in the new front parlor. The sweeping cove between wall and ceiling is punctuated by the ornate woodwork above the windows. The mirror reflects the oak doors leading from the foyer and makes the narrow room feel spacious.

reason "brownstone" is interchangeable with "row house," a more pedestrian way to describe the housing style. And this house, despite the ornate details inside, was a modest building designed for families of modest income. The renovation we were about to undertake would continue that tradition.

Karen and Kevin wanted to build a home for their family but needed some rental income to help pay for the recent purchase and pending renovation. The plan was to renovate the first and second floors for their family and then to create two rental apartments, one on the top floor and another on the garden level. Their two older sons would share a bedroom on the third floor and the baby would sleep in an alcove next to the new master bedroom. Karen and Kevin hoped to take back the top floor in about five years, after replenishing their savings and paying off some of the mortgage, so their family could spread out.

When work began, we focused our efforts on the owner's unit. We quickly did away with the nine apartments by taking down walls and closing off hallway doors. On the first floor, the separate back and front apartments became an open floor plan that ran from an elegant parlor in the front to a bright new kitchen in the rear. We restored the old fretwork and used it to separate the new parlor from an adjacent den, and beyond that a small dining area filled with plenty of light, thanks to its southern exposure and the new windows that were no longer wrapped in wrought-iron burglar bars.

When the building served as a rooming house, tenants moved from floor to floor using a four-story staircase on the left side of the building. Tenants and

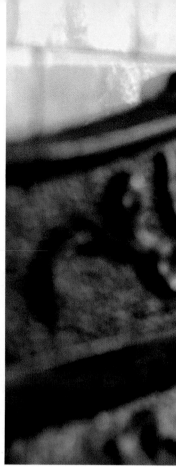

RIGHT: Traditionally, brownstones had two sets of entry doors. On warmer days the outer set might be left open, inviting neighbors to drop in. Our outer doors have a hinged glass panel behind the ornamental ironwork that let in breezes—but not unexpected guests.

FACING PAGE, TOP AND BOTTOM LEFT: There was at least one fireplace on every floor and they were all ornate. Some were decorated with mirrors or oak surrounds and some were adorned with cast-iron plates like these. At one time, these fireboxes were the home's only source of heat; today, they add warmth in other ways.

FACING PAGE, TOP RIGHT: One of my favorite details in the original house was the plaster cove moulding with its broad sweep up the wall. It was severely damaged when the building was converted to a rooming house, but we were able to restore it with the help of a local plasterer from nearby Red Hook, Brooklyn.

FACING PAGE, BOTTOM RIGHT: We were lucky that many of the original ornate brass doorknobs and hinges remained intact and only needed modest refurbishing. A salvage yard was our source for missing hardware.

guests shared the front door and passed each other in this common hallway as they came and went. Since there would still be two rental units in the building after renovations, the staircase would remain a shared public space. But Karen and Kevin wanted some privacy too. They wanted to move from their bedrooms on the second floor to their kitchen and living room on the first floor and to the laundry room and guest bedroom carved out of the garden apartment on the ground floor. So we restored an old set of stairs that led from the first floor to the basement. To connect the first and second floors, our contractor, Mike Streaman, cut a four-foot-square hole in the ceiling and installed a metal staircase that Karen and Kevin purchased online from a favorite local website, Brownstoners.com. The iron stair, with its triangular treads spiraling up about eleven feet, became not just the signature feature of the main room but also represented Karen and Kevin's effort to recycle, restore, and reuse as many period features as possible.

Much of the finer restoration work fell on the shoulders of John Thomas, a soft-spoken artist who painstakingly restored room after room of original woodwork. John used his artist's touch and nearly inexhaustible patience to clean, stain, patch, and paint just about all of the woodwork in the building—the paneled wainscoting,

LEFT: A rental unit on the top floor is the brightest in the house and set off a debate among the crew over whether they would rather live upstairs or in the garden apartment, with its views of the private backyard. It was a tough choice, but I preferred the unit on the top floor.

RIGHT: Period details on every floor and in every room, like this fireplace, were a major reason that the homeowners bought the house despite its state of total disrepair.

FACING PAGE: The homeowners purchased this metal spiral staircase online and made it the focal point in the first-floor sitting area. It allows the family to move between their two floors without using the public stairway.

eight-foot-high oak-veneered doors, the Italianate fretwork, and the floor-to-ceiling maple cabinets in the new master bedroom. John is an alchemist and used homemade concoctions of dyes, stains, and gels to restore a piece of wood to its original richness or to cover years of neglect with his hand-applied interpretations of wood grain that fooled everyone who laid eyes on his work.

John Thomas was just one of the tradesmen who worked with Mike Streaman. The plumbing and heating system was the domain of Randy and Eric Gitli—plumbers, brothers, and, to our delight, lifelong fans of the show. Not long into the project, the Gitlis shared with us an old home video they had made as teenagers, featuring the two of them walking though their mother's home, playing the roles of plumber and homeowner in a parody of *This Old House*. It was hilarious to hear two Brooklyn boys, with their acid-washed jeans and

BELOW: We placed
the kitchen in the
back of the house,
overlooking the
garden. The crisp
lines of the painted
cabinets, traditional
and modern at the
same time, set the
tone for the rest of
the décor.

mulletlike haircuts, attempt Boston accents. As we all laughed at their good nature (and bad accents), we knew we were in good hands. Vinny Verderosa updated the building's antiquated electrical system, a huge project he managed to pull off almost silently in the background of our chaotic job site. We only heard from Vinny when we pulled him into scenes for the television show or when his infectious laugh rolled through the brownstone.

Mike and his team are fiercely loyal to Brooklyn. They work almost exclusively in the borough and pride themselves on how infrequently they cross the bridge to "the other side." And because they work so frequently in Brooklyn, they also work on lots of brownstones—it's unavoidable. Their affection for their hometown and its brownstones is contagious, and it was inspiring to see them cram ten months of exquisite restoration work into six intense months to meet our television schedule.

The result was impressive; when we were finished, the old rooming house was completely transformed. We pieced back together the once chopped-up building and ended up with three kitchens, four bathrooms, and six bedrooms in three distinct units. The rental unit on the garden level was reminiscent of the original house, with restored wainscoting and a handsome fireplace, while the rental unit on the top floor had a crisp and clean look, with plenty of sunlight, bright walls, and light-colored oak floors. And in the center was Karen and Kevin's new home. All of the original details that they loved and that Mike Streaman's team restored gave the house an unmistakable elegance. It was almost imposing to walk through the restored entry door, with it masculine oak veneer and substantial brass doorknobs. But inside, the home now had a warm, informal feel, thanks to a new, open floor plan that allowed easy flow and interior views from the front to the back of the house.

For a century our brownstone had been reconceived and repurposed by its many occupants, whether they were families, tenants, or landlords. And in 2008, the house was again transformed to serve the needs of new owners. It was now Karen and Kevin's turn to make this little corner of Brooklyn their home.

LEFT: Brownstones often have windows only on the front and back since their side walls are shared by neighboring buildings, so it's essential to let light in wherever possible, even if it means having a window in the shower. Encasing it in tile helps prevent water damage.

RIGHT: Even the simplest closet doors had great details like beaded mouldings and maple panels between oak stiles and rails. We used reproduction doorknobs and backplates wherever the originals were missing.

Close Up

Stephen "Dino" D'Onofrio

Ginger Rogers had it easy. Sure, Fred Astaire's legendary partner had to dance backwards and in high heels, but at least she was on a dance floor—a flat, wide-open dance floor. There are no flat, wide-open areas on a job site; only piles of dirt, muddy holes, and lumber strewn about, ready to trip even the most careful workers. It's a tough place to work and an even tougher place to film, but our cameraman, Dino, makes it look easy.

Most television shows employ at least two cameramen to capture scenes from different angles; an audio technician to adjust sound levels and carry boom mikes; and grips and gaffers to run cords and adjust lights. But *This Old House* doesn't have to bother with all that, because we have Dino. Dino does it all: He has an earpiece so he can listen to the on-camera talent and the director simultaneously. He has up to four audio receivers cleverly strapped to the back of his camera. He keeps one eye on his subjects and the other eye in the camera, monitoring things like white balance, iris, focus, and audio levels. And he alone captures every second of the show with a single twenty-pound camera. It's like dancing backwards—only with multiple partners, the weight of a small child on your shoulder, and a television control room in your head.

During one shoot, Dino was filming on the roof of a four-story townhouse when the skies opened, raining on the camera lens and making the roof as slippery as ice. What did Dino do? He kept filming and, while walking backward, reached into his pocket, pulled out a handkerchief, and wiped the lens clean. He never missed a frame, and the camera didn't shake a bit. Now *that's* dancing.

05. WESTON TIMBER FRAME

Pete and Amy Favat are true creative types. They both have backgrounds in advertising—in fact Pete is the creative director at a large national advertising agency. The couple was full of original ideas that spilled out in the form of sketches and pictures and short videos on their laptops, and they used their creative powers to dream up ways to improve their house. By contrast, the house they lived in seemed, well, uninspired at best. It was built in the 1970s, was rather plain, and certainly didn't appear to be designed either by or for people bursting with creative energy. Its gambrel roof slumped over the narrow second floor and hung just a little too low, making the whole building seem squat and lazy.

BEFORE

LEFT: This 1970s house did not inspire its homeowners, who decided it needed to come down to make way for their dream house.

FACING PAGE: We avoided traditional demolition and instead took the home apart in a process called "deconstruction." Here, the original foundation is picked clean and the chimney is about to come down, its bricks slated to be reused or recycled along with 85% of the home's original material.

RIGHT: Much of the home was prefabricated in New Hampshire. Packed flat, then wrapped, the timber frame and wall panels were shipped one hundred miles to the job site on several trucks.

BELOW: The frame of the house, made of precut post and beams, was braced in place during assembly.

The inside was dim, with wide knotty-pine floors, stained wainscoting on the walls, and dark beams crisscrossing the ceiling in a failed attempt to give the house some grandeur. When I first met Pete and Amy and listened to all their ideas and felt the buzz of their creativity, it was clear they were out of place in their drab 1970s house. They knew it, and they wanted a change.

When it comes to where we live, most of us have no problem identifying the things we *don't* like. Making the list of exactly what we *do* like is the bigger challenge. Fortunately for us, Pete and Amy knew exactly what they liked and what they wanted. First, they wanted to stay put. They loved the town in which they live: its proximity to Boston, its great schools, and all the friends they had made there over the years. And even though the front of their house

looked out over a busy road, their acre of land was a great piece of property. The house sat high up on a hill and the backyard sloped down to a stream and adjacent wetlands. It was a great place for kids, and each morning on their way to the bus stop the Favats' young son and daughter crossed the creek on a small wooden bridge Pete had built for them. On weekends, the kids would search for turtles in the fast-moving water of the creek or for hawks and the occasional owl in the tall trees growing in the wetlands that covered nearly half of their property. The other half was covered by narrow trails winding through high, thick bushes, some grass to lounge on, and a large raised garden, also built by the Favats, which produced vegetables that ended up on their dinner table.

LEFT: A crane does the heavy work, lifting the home's timber skeleton onto the floor deck. Bents that run the length of the house were assembled in the shop or on-site and then lifted into place as one piece.

RIGHT: In a departure from conventional timber framing, Tedd Benson assembles the wall panels beforehand—complete with structural studs, sheathing, insulation, and windows—and then hoists them onto the timber frame. Construction of the home's frame and shell took just weeks instead of months.

AFTER

The second thing Pete and Amy knew they wanted was to build their dream house. While on a ski vacation in Idaho they had stayed in a timber-frame cabin—the kind with lots of exposed wood and large wooden beams held up by even larger posts. They appreciated the rustic style and the craftsmanship always on display in a timber-frame house, but mostly they loved that the house reminded them they were on vacation. It was during that trip that it dawned on them that their dream house was one that would make them feel as if they were on vacation every day. But Pete and Amy knew there was no way their current house could ever inspire that feeling. For them to build their dream house, the old one had to go, and that led to their third wish—instead of throwing away their old house, they wanted to give it away.

Making the pieces of that complicated puzzle work—staying put on their property while feeling like they were on vacation; building a new house without simply tearing down the old one—would be no simple task, not even for *This Old House*. To get the job done we needed to build a team.

Our first partner was a nonprofit organization called Restore, which specializes in *deconstruction*, the process of dismantling a house piece by piece instead of smashing it to the ground with a bulldozer. Restore's small crew took apart the

FACING PAGE:
The lower-level mudroom is full of rich details and wrapped in wood that masks the home's prefabricated pedigree. An antique bench beside the door feels like it's always been in the new house.

ABOVE LEFT:
The fireplace, with its raised hearth, takes center stage in the dining room and can be enjoyed from the whole first floor. A small door to the left opens to the outdoors, making it easy to restock the woodpile.

ABOVE RIGHT:
A newel post is cleverly capped with a reproduction industrial light.

RIGHT: A metal staircase with wood treads runs through the center of the house. The homeowners' creative flair is evident in their choice of signs: one neon and one from the A&P supermarket. It's no coincidence: The homeowners' names are Amy and Pete.

FACING PAGE: Tedd Benson's team also made the handcrafted front door, complete with bull's-eye glass. The low ceiling above the entryway provides intimacy and prepares you for the dramatic three-story stairwell capped with a cupola.

Favats' house, starting with the obvious pieces like windows and doors that are easily reused. They worked their way through the home's layers, removing kitchen cabinets and light fixtures, then the hardwood floors and moldings. They pulled off the cedar clapboards and the plywood sheathing; they dismantled the two-by-four framing studs and then the larger floor joists and roof rafters. The crew of four pulled nails from the wood and removed fiberglass insulation, even taking out the copper wire that ran behind the walls from switches to outlets.

As piece after piece of material was liberated from the house, it was stacked neatly in the driveway. As I looked at those piles, it occurred to me they must be similar to the piles of materials that had been stacked on the property forty years earlier when the house was first built, proof that these items had a lot of life left

ABOVE: Traditional features, such as the chrome faucet and barn-board siding, are offset by a concrete countertop in this powder room. The homeowners opted for a smooth, polished look and molded bowl, a shape repeated in the master bath (pictured on next page).

in them. After about a month of picking and stacking, the Restore crew loaded everything onto a truck and shipped it to the their retail facility, so contractors and homeowners could buy the lumber, cabinets, and copper for a fraction of their original costs and use them again on new houses or renovations. Any materials that weren't reused were recycled, like the concrete foundation that was pulverized into aggregate and used as base material for new roads. When all was said and done, 85 percent of Pete and Amy's house was either reused or recycled. They effectively gave their house away to hundreds of people in thousands of pieces.

Tedd Benson was our second collaborator. Tedd builds timber-frame homes, and to us, he was more like an old friend than a partner. He had collaborated with *This Old House* on many occasions going back more than twenty years, most memorably in 1989 when he helped us build the "Concord Barn," a new home for the Wickwire family. As one of the foremost timber framers in the country, Tedd was already known to Pete and Amy, who loved his style of homes and his easygoing manner. It was left to Tedd and his team to design and prefabricate the house.

Timber framing, Tedd will tell you, has been practiced for centuries and has always been about prefabrication. Large pieces of wood are cut and shaped on the ground, prefitted with mortises and tenons that form the joinery, and assembled and raised in short order once the prefabrication is complete. Traditional timber framing primarily concerns itself with the building's frame or its skeleton, while the other parts—the floors, the walls, the interior details—are usually added later using conventional on-site building methods. Thus most timber-framed buildings are a mix of prefabrication and site-built techniques.

But not Tedd's buildings. He has taken the concept of prefabrication to new levels: Just about the entire Favat house was built off-site in a large workshop in Walpole, New Hampshire. Computer-drafted architectural drawings were sent to another computer controlling a large CNC machine that measured and cut

BELOW LEFT: A single-piece concrete countertop sits on top of the double vanity in the master bath. The distinctly formed bowl is a custom shape molded into the counter.

BELOW RIGHT: Most of the walls in the house are exposed wood, but smooth, neutral surfaces like plaster and tile were used in the master bath.

ten-inch-thick Douglas fir beams, then hollowed out mortises with carbide-tipped bits and used fast-spinning cutting wheels to shape tenons with incredible precision. The same machine measured and cut pine two-by-fours, minimizing waste in a way that couldn't be matched by even the finest carpenters working on a job site. Tedd's crew also prefabricated the walls in the shop, not just applying sheathing to two-by-four frames but running electrical wiring and plumbing between the wall's layers, injecting cellulose, and installing windows complete with waterproofing and exterior trim. They nailed cedar shingles to the wall's exteriors and even hung drywall and wainscoting on its interior. The prefabrication was so thorough that the building's mechanical room—complete with boiler, pumps, piping, and valves—was entirely built in the New Hampshire workshop. Then all of the pieces—the walls, roof, floors, and frame—were laid flat on a truck and shipped to the Favats' address. Over the course of a few weeks, the crew craned into place and assembled every prefabricated piece, in a modern-day cousin to an old-fashioned barn raising.

The house was by no means finished when Tedd and his crew completed their on-site assembly. The prefabrication of houses, even as far as Tedd Benson has taken the process, has a way to go before it looks anything like the assembly of a car, where piles of metal parts are assembled within hours and roll off the line

FACING PAGE
UPPER LEFT: The reinterpreted Dutch door leads to a back porch; while most of the house is clad in cedar shingles, here we used antique barn boards.

UPPER RIGHT: The kitchen is a collection of materials: wooden beams and paneling, stainless steel fixtures, concrete countertops, and painted cabinets. A small pantry sits behind the wall oven.

LOWER: A reproduction mechanic's light hangs upside down above the office desk; it's just one of many antique industrial lights favored by the homeowners.

LEFT: Old tractor seats were turned into kitchen stools by Dick Silva.

BELOW LEFT: A custom-made copper owl sits atop the home's cupola.

BELOW RIGHT: The dining-room table is on wheels that slide on hidden floor tracks. The table can be rolled close to the fireplace for an intimate dinner for two or away from it to accommodate a Thanksgiving crowd.

LIVE OAK

Four "crucks" brace the corners of the dining room—these are naturally curved trees, split in half and then inclined toward one another. You can see them in the adjacent picture. It's a centuries-old timber-framing technique, but in this case, the wood is actually an artifact of the region's once-thriving shipbuilding industry.

The crucks are made of live oak, a semi-evergreen tree in the beech family that was highly coveted by shipwrights in the late eighteenth century. Live oak is the heaviest of all oaks, and its tensile strength and resistance to rot made it ideal for wooden shipbuilding. But it was sought out mostly for its shape. Live oak doesn't grow long or straight, making it a poor choice for lumber; instead, its thick branches spread low on the trunk with natural curves that mimic the arched ribs, or futtocks, of a ship's frame. Live oak was such an important component of wooden shipbuilding in the late eighteenth and early nineteenth centuries that an entire industry was dedicated to getting it from forest to shipyard.

Live oak grows near the coast from Virginia to Texas, and each winter, crews would sail to these southern forests to harvest the mighty trees. It was a time when many wooden ships were built without the help of drawings; instead, they were imagined in a master builder's mind then designed, literally, by rule of thumb. So instead of southern loggers doing the work, New England shipwrights would sail south carrying ship plans in their heads and templates in their hands in search of the perfect tree or branch. The trees were then felled by hand, hauled by oxen, loaded on ships and sailed back to the great northern shipyards, including Boston, where our four timbers ended up.

Once the live oak was in the yard, a shipwright would shape the timbers into the thousands of pieces needed to build a ship, label them, and then sink them into a pool of briny water that preserved and hardened the wood. There they lay until it was time to assemble a new ship, something that happened frequently—the average life of a sailing ship in those days was a mere ten years.

For reasons unknown, our four pieces (and many others) were long ago forgotten and lost. They sat submerged near Boston's Charlestown Navy Yard for nearly two hundred years, perfectly preserved, until they were discovered during a development project. A swampy patch of land was being converted into a parking lot and the ancient timbers were discovered during the dredging process.

Most people in the wood salvage business know Tedd Benson, and sure enough, when these timbers were discovered, Tedd got the call. He bought the best of the lot, about eighteen pieces once slated for a ship's bow. When Tedd told our homeowners what he had they leaped at the opportunity to make four of them the centerpiece of their home. Today, easily five-hundred years old, these live oak crucks stand in tribute to the shipbuilding industry that once defined a region and to the craft of timber framing celebrated by this home. ✧

ready to drive. The house still needed many months of work from Tom Silva and his tradesmen to complete the effect the homeowners desired. And that effect reflected all of Pete and Amy's creativity, which was no longer bound by the low roof and dark corners of their old house. With the help of Tedd and Tommy, the Favats' dream came together, and they designed a house unlike anything I'd ever seen before. There was wood everywhere: on the floors, walls, ceiling, windows, doors, and posts and beams throughout. They added other materials: a metal staircase that ran through the center of the house, concrete countertops in the kitchen and master bathroom, and a corrugated metal skin on a second-floor wall (the metal was salvaged by Tom's brother, Dick Silva, from a dilapidated commercial building).

Pete and Amy added rich and whimsical details, like worn metal tractor seats turned into kitchen island stools and old industrial light fixtures that illuminated the eclectic mix of materials. They picked fieldstone for the oversized fireplace in the center of the house and had Tedd's crew build a custom dining-room table, complete with metal wheels that ran on concealed tracks. Outside, they added a deep fire pit

BELOW LEFT: We harvested trees from a local forest and used them as rafters in the guest bedroom, shown here.

BELOW RIGHT: Reproduction pendant lights inspired by the factory floor hang over the kitchen island.

FACING PAGE: Concrete has infinite design possibilities. In the kitchen, the homeowners chose a dark color and molded basin rather than an opening to receive an undermount sink. The drain board was also designed into the concrete form for an integrated look.

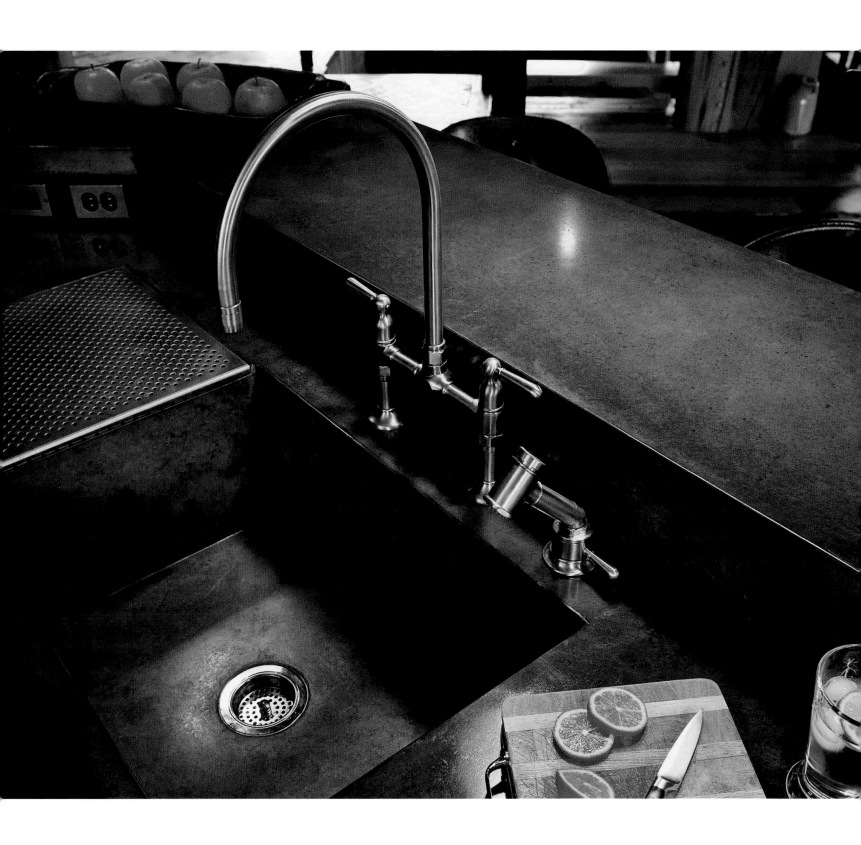

and more metal stairs designed to let heavy winter snow fall through the iron web of the stair's tread—other ideas from the Idaho ski vacation.

In the end, Pete and Amy were granted their three wishes. They stayed on their property with its brook and sprawling wetlands. They gave away their old house, saving it from the landfill and making sure it was properly reused. And they built their dream house, filled with exposed wooden posts and beams and eclectic details throughout. And whether you sat by the fireplace inside or the fire pit outside, or if you walked through the front door and into the light streaming through a three-story-high cupola, it was easy to feel as if you were in a mountain lodge enjoying a well-deserved vacation. For Pete and Amy, it was a feeling they could enjoy every day in their new house.

FACING PAGE: This picture reveals a great deal about how the house was constructed. The knee brace running in front of the window is part of a wooden frame that was entirely assembled before it was "wrapped" with prefabricated wall panels. The walls are like skin on a post-and-beam skeleton.

ABOVE: We painted the mudroom walls red and then lightly removed some of the color to create an aged look, but there's nothing old-fashioned about the media room tucked behind the double doors.

Close Up
Tedd Benson

"**O**nward.**"** Tedd Benson signs his e-mails with that word, and not just the important e-mails—all of them. He's been signing his correspondence that way for twenty-five years: an urgent plea slipped into every message. But it's more than just a plea—it's a philosophy. Tedd believes in constant improvement and forward progress, and he believes there must be a better way to build houses.

While Tedd practices the ancient art of timber framing, he's still looking to change the future of housing. His craftsmen use chisels and draw knives, shape mortises and tenons, but they also use computers, sophisticated milling machines, and lean manufacturing techniques more commonly found in advanced assembly plants throughout the world. This is all in pursuit of building an energy-efficient, sustainable, and affordable prefabricated home—which is a lot harder than it sounds.

Most houses are built by tradesmen working together to assemble tens of thousands of parts, including lumber, plaster, and pipes. Materials are shipped to a job site, exposed to the elements, and then shaped and fitted, mostly by hand. Compared to the production of cars or computers, traditional housing construction is quite inefficient.

Tedd has refined this process by changing the building site, as he says, "from a place of inefficient manufacturing to a place of efficient assembly." His homes are manufactured in a workshop under controlled conditions and then assembled quickly and efficiently on the job site. And even though Tedd's homes easily outperform the conventional alternative, he's still looking ahead—to create a house that will last five hundred years, require zero energy for heat and power, and still be affordable. He admits it's an "audacious" goal but he knows the direction in which we must travel in order to succeed. It's the only way Tedd travels: *Onward—onward*.

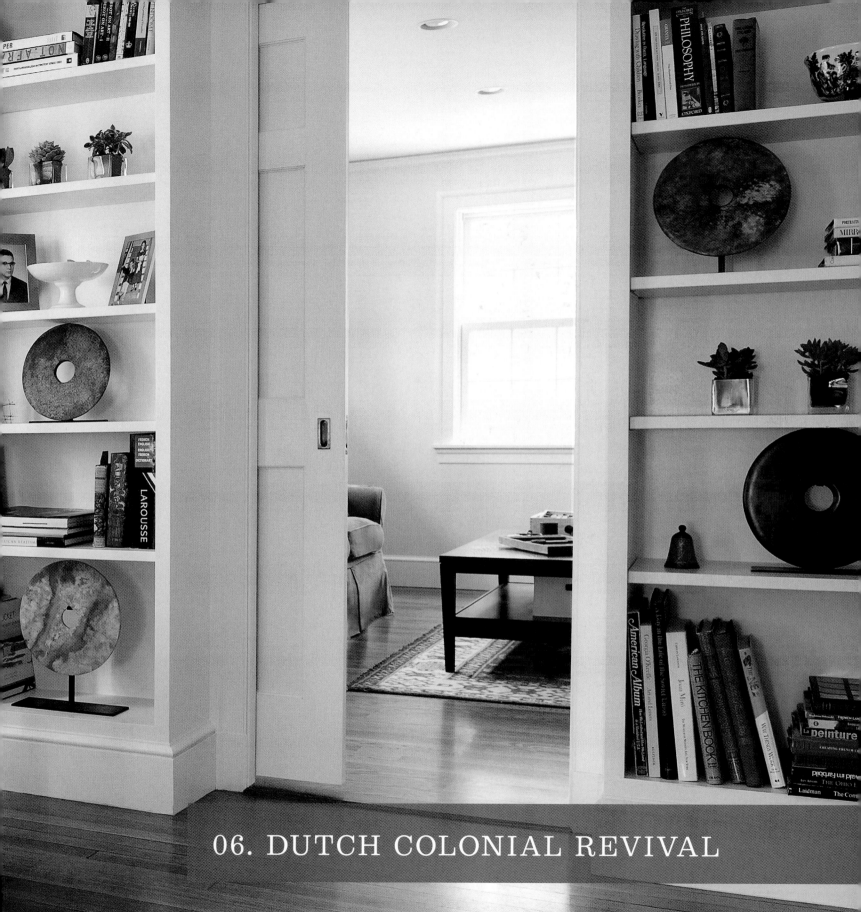

06. DUTCH COLONIAL REVIVAL

There's never one single reason we choose a project house. Sometimes it's the story line, or the homeowners, or the location, but most of the time it's a combination of all of these reasons and more. The decision process is more of an art than a science and it's a collaborative effort—primarily between the production team and the general contractor, Tom Silva. In the case of our house in Newton Center the consensus for our decision was a familiar one: a modest-size project for a family on a budget, their desire for a little more space, a tired kitchen in need of updating, and so on. These are all good reasons, but none of them interested me as much as the style of the house: It was a Dutch Colonial Revival, and believe it or not, I was taken with its roof.

BEFORE

LEFT: The homeowners had previously added built-in bookcases on the stairway landing, a precursor to their dream of a full library.

FACING PAGE: The home was built in 1915. We stripped off the three-season porch to make way for a new addition.

ABOVE: The original kitchen was cramped for a family of four; the stove had one working burner, there were no upper cabinets, and storage was limited.

FACING PAGE, TOP: With some of the kitchen walls taken down, you can see the "stairway to nowhere." It had been capped at some point in the past and the homeowners were using it as a pantry.

FACING PAGE, INSET: A foam model of the final plan. Note the new addition where the three-season porch once was, as well as the symmetry of the gambrel roofs.

This particular Dutch Colonial had been built in 1915, and it had that form's iconic feature—the gambrel roof. The gambrel is a broken roof line, where an upper roof with a shallow pitch intersects a lower roof with a steeper pitch. The look is unmistakable and the purpose, or at least one of its purposes, is to add headroom and living space to the attic, which is effectively the second floor. As odd as it may sound, that's what excited me about this house. It was part novelty and part curiosity: I had never worked on this style of house before, and dealing with a gambrel poses design challenges and offers some desirable features. I was curious to see how we handled this. More on that later, because as much as our homeowners liked the style of their house, there was plenty they didn't like—and they were determined to transform it.

Bill and Gillian Pierce had lived in the house with their two young children and their golden retriever for five years before we arrived. Their plans for the renovation included a new kitchen, the conversion of a small two-season sunporch into additional year-round living space, a new office/guest bedroom, and the addition of a library area at the top of the stairs. In total only about 330 square feet would be added and about half of the original house would remain untouched, but once complete, the renovation would entirely change how the family used the house.

The kitchen wasn't decrepit but it did have some challenges, including a bathroom immediately adjacent to the kitchen table, which was too small for Bill, Gillian, and their two children; an old staircase that led nowhere but provided needed storage space for pots, pans, and dry goods; and an old stove with only one

AFTER

working burner. The remedy was, as it often is, to gut the space, enlarge it, create a proper entryway and better circulation, and add lots of windows and the usual accompaniment of modern appliances and lighting.

As *This Old House* projects go, the work in the kitchen was pretty standard fare, but what made it unusual this time around was the fact that the Pierce family did not move out during the renovation! They hunkered down and lived through the dust and the disturbances that are abundant when a crew of twenty or so tears apart and rebuilds your house around you. Each morning as we arrived to film episodes of our show, the family walked the dog, the kids headed off to school, then the house was ours again—but only for about eight hours. In the late afternoon, the family would return to the few barely inhabitable spaces left in the house, including the basement, which served as a temporary kitchen and was now home to that one-burner stove.

One afternoon, as we demolished the kitchen with the help of the homeowners, I asked Bill about their decision to stay in the house during our messy invasion. His simple answer spoke volumes: "Know your house, love your house." He and Gillian believed that getting dirty during the renovation, either intentionally or not, and seeing the bones of their house revealed, restored, and then put back together again would increase their appreciation for their home. And I have no doubt it did.

FACING PAGE: The homeowners got their dream library. The stairway landing was pushed back into the addition; a new office is tucked out of sight beyond this comfortable sitting area.

ABOVE: The kitchen is no longer cramped for the family of four. A new dining area is wrapped with glass and looks out onto the small but newly landscaped backyard.

THE GAMBREL ROOF AND
THE DUTCH COLONIAL

When I renovated my first house, I took over unfinished attic space and turned it into three bedrooms and a bathroom. I did this with the help of two new dormers and nine new windows. The rooms were small but cozy, and were made more so by all the angles of the roof that defined the ceilings in each room. And there were plenty of angles! The roof had three different hips and four separate dormers, so there wasn't a flat ceiling anywhere to be found. When my family and I moved out of that house after living there for eight years, I missed the low, clipped ceilings of my converted attic and found the full-height bedroom ceilings of my new house plain and unsatisfying. There's something comforting about a bedroom tucked up under the roof, and when you live in a Dutch Colonial that's where the bedrooms are—right under the roof.

Architect and author Russell Versaci says the Dutch Colonial style owes as much to the English as it does to the Dutch. In Holland, the primary building material was brick. The distinctive architectural feature of a traditional Dutch house "was a roof that projected out two feet or more in front and back and was gracefully curved at the eaves," says Versaci. That is to say that the traditional Dutch house was not made of wood and did not have a gambrel roof. The gambrel, as Versaci points out in his book *Roots of Home*, was an English feature commonly found on barns in the English countryside. It only became part of Dutch homes in America when colonists from Holland and England lived side by side in and around the Hudson Valley.

Today the gambrel roof is synonymous with Dutch Colonial, and I've heard many theories about why gambrel roofs were invented. Some believe farmers used them on their barns to add additional storage for hay, and the fact that they are commonly found on farmsteads suggests there is a lot of truth to this. Others speculate that the gambrel roof was invented to avoid taxes at a time when homes were assessed by their number of stories. Since it's common for the entire second floor of a Dutch Colonial to be shingled, one could make the argument that the top story is nothing more than an attic and should not result in a higher levy. And then there's the idea that the gambrel roof was a simple way to add additional headspace in an attic, which it certainly is.

The reason gambrels were invented may be in dispute, but the effect of this roof style is not. When tucked up under the broken pitch of the gambrel, you can't help but feel protected and comfortable. ⊗

Bill, a writer and editor of a literary magazine, and Gillian, a college professor, love books and are around them all day. So when they moved into their house, Bill, with his father's help, installed a wall of bookshelves at the top of the staircase. It was their version of a library. They loved it and they wanted more. So, off the back of the house, where the old sunporch once stood, we built a new two-story addition. Upstairs, it would house a new office (the home's second) so both Bill and Gillian could work at home. To get to the new space you now pass through yet another new room, a proper library that is about ten feet deep and eight feet wide. It is lined with shelves on two walls, has a built-in bench and a large window on the third wall, and, just as it had been before, is set prominently atop the stairs so that a wall of books once again greets everyone who enters through the front door.

A two-story addition to a Dutch colonial with its gambrel roof is not a simple assignment. The roof line can easily be broken by dormers, and it often is. But adding a new roof that sits atop a new addition to an existing gambrel can go badly, fast. Enter Paul Rovinelli, our architect. Fortunately for Bill and Gillian, Paul had lived in and renovated his own Dutch Colonial and had renovated another one just across the street from our project house. In each case he deftly married a new gambrel roof line into an old one, and he would do it again for us. The solution, in its most basic sense, was to set the addition at ninety degrees to the original house, so that the new roof was distinct and separate. This helped prevent the various roof lines

PREVIOUS PAGE: From the foot of the stairs you can see the new library on the stairway landing and on through to the new back door. You must pass under a new curved ceiling in the alcove that separates old from new.

FACING PAGE: The addition made space for a second office. Just a hint of the gambrel roof's underside is seen in the corner, but that's all it takes to convey a sense of comfort.

ABOVE: The library is as much for sitting as it is for books. We made room for storage underneath and artwork on the walls, and the large window ensures that there is plenty of natural light.

PREVIOUS PAGE, LEFT: The home- owners fretted endlessly over the position of the kitchen island—no doubt a result of living in tight quarters for years—to make sure there was proper clearance for the refrigerator and oven doors.

PREVIOUS PAGE, RIGHT: We hardly touched the front of the house; old meets new where the pantry sits adjacent to the new kitchen. The pantry's wooden counter has as much charm as the kitchen's stone counter has style.

from being muddled and it also replicated an adjacent wing of the house, giving the building a new level of symmetry.

The renovation was completed with some work to the exterior. We stripped off the home's vinyl siding and restored the wooden clapboards underneath. The claps were in remarkably good shape, suggesting that a previous owner wasn't concerned with their condition but simply tired of repainting them. We installed a new driveway and carted away an old garage, building a new one in its place. Landscape contractor Roger Cook, with the help of the homeowners and their family and friends, laid down a new brick patio that connected to the new kitchen via a proper entrance. And while we didn't do much to the basement, we did remove that old stove and its one working burner. Then we removed ourselves because, as Bill and Gillian found out, knowing your house may help you to love it, but ridding your house of both a construction and a television crew ensures that you can enjoy it.

FACING PAGE: The second home office, located off the library, is a hidden treat.

ABOVE LEFT: The kitchen is now large enough for the entire family and will likely be the room of choice for meals, despite the home's comfortable dining room.

Close Up
Deborah Hood

Deborah Hood's official title is senior series producer, and it's a fitting one, given her resumé and day-to-day responsibilities. Her television background is broad, with network experience at HBO, Discovery, Lifetime Television, and others, and she's worked with several television formats, from the talk show to the two-hour special to independent documentaries. Deb's great at what she does—she won an Emmy in 2007—and as her title suggests, she's intimately involved with making our show: coordinating shoot days, corralling on-air talent, writing scripts and outlines, sitting with video editors, and collaborating with directors.

But what Deb's title does not indicate is that she does as much to get our houses built as she does to chronicle the process. Renovating a house is a complicated and stressful endeavor; doing it in half the normal time on national television makes it even more so. And while Tom Silva, our general contractor has primary responsibility for the job site, Deb works by his side every day. "Project manager" should be added to her title.

Deb is constantly looking for content, and that means identifying new technologies and materials. It also means that our building supplies don't always come from the lumberyard; they often come directly from manufacturers, accompanied by a product manager eager to explain his wares and a public-relations department eager to manage their message. Deb filters all of it and must act as liaison between architect, designer, and builder. She also gently holds homeowners' hands through the thousands of decisions that go into every renovation, while firmly encouraging them to favor the decisions that will keep a project on budget and on schedule. She's a producer and a project manager—and maybe a "miracle worker" too.

07. SHINGLE-STYLE VICTORIAN

"**M**ove or improve?" It's a question many people face as their families grow and their dreams change. And it was exactly the question Paul Friedberg and Maddy Krauss wrestled with as they looked around the modest Colonial house in which they had lived for ten years. Outside was a big backyard, perfectly flat and with plenty of play space for their two young sons and the neighborhood friends who often stopped by. The yard was so inviting that on the first day I met the family I found myself deep in a game of stickball with Paul and Maddy's youngest son instead of filming a scene with his parents about their current dilemma.

BEFORE

FACING PAGE: Our shingle-style Victorian was built in 1897 during the heyday of the style; it was grand on the outside, with its wraparound front porch, and elegant on the inside, with oak-paneled rooms, but it was outdated and ready for a renovation.

ABOVE LEFT: The entry hall was grand even before we touched it. It featured stained glass, oak wainscoting, and sweeping curves along the staircase.

ABOVE RIGHT: The back of the house was plain and inaccessible—anything but grand. We jacked up one corner to restructure it, making way for a new back porch, staircase, and patio.

FACING PAGE LEFT: All of the exterior work was relegated to the rear. Here, we are adding a new covered porch off the kitchen and new windows for the master suite on the second floor.

FACING PAGE RIGHT: New fleurs-de-lis are cast for repairs to the stained-glass windows.

The yard was perfect, but inside, the house was cramped. The kitchen was in good shape but could not easily accommodate the friends, family, and neighbors who visited frequently. Paul and Maddy thought about building an addition off the back of the house. An addition would give them the space they needed and allow them to stay in the neighborhood, but they worried about overimproving the house. They even went so far as to ask a neighbor, a well-respected architect, to give them some ideas. At the same time, they kept their eyes on the real-estate market, which is how they eventually solved the overriding question: "Move or improve?" The answer, for Paul and Maddy, turned out to be "move *and* improve."

They bought a house that had plenty of space and was a bit grander—just two blocks away. It was a large, shingle-style house, a classic New England

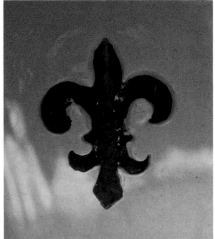

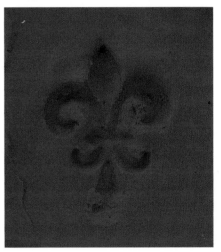

style often associated with summer homes and breezy waterfront living. This particular house wasn't near the ocean, but when it was built atop a hill in Newton, Massachusetts, in the late nineteenth century, it was definitely considered a "getaway" from bustling, dirty downtown Boston. Constructed in 1897 during the heyday of the shingle-style movement, the house had just about every signature feature of this architectural style. Cedar shingles, instead of the corner boards and trim traditionally found on most houses, covered its exterior in a continuous wrap. A large porch ran across the front and side of the house, deep enough for the whole family and then some to enjoy a meal and take in the summer breeze. The home's entryway was wide and inviting and quickly led visitors into a sprawling foyer where an oversized central staircase, wrapped in an elegant oak balustrade, gently wound its way up to the second floor. Rich

AFTER

wainscoting in the foyer and several interior and exterior windows made of leaded and stained glass lent the home a level of formality one would expect from proper Victorians of the day.

The home's grandeur and Victorian sensibility appealed to Paul and Maddy as much as it concerned them. While the front parlor was fit to receive the minister, for example, the kitchen was better outfitted for the maid. In typical Victorian fashion, the "working side" of the house—kitchen, pantry, and bathroom—was a warren of small, dark, uninviting rooms built for function and nothing more. But Paul and Maddy didn't have any servants, and they certainly didn't want to be relegated to a kitchen more cramped than their last. And so their plan to "move" became a plan to "improve" as well.

Paul and Maddy hired Treff Lafleche, the same neighbor and architect who had advised them on a possible addition to their little Colonial, to plan a major renovation of their new shingle-style Victorian. Treff started by completely redesigning how the house would be used. The front of the house would remain elegant and stately. Oak wainscoting and stained-glass windows would be restored instead of removed. The front parlor would stay and an adjacent living

FACING PAGE: The rear of the house is finally accessible, and the covered porch off the kitchen and the stairs leading down to the patio are now appropriately wrapped in shingles. The retaining walls, made of fieldstone, are offset by the crisp lines and geometric patterns of the bluestone.

ABOVE LEFT: Several oak fireplace surrounds and mantels were restored to their original splendor.

ABOVE RIGHT: The new entrance off the back of the house sits between the kitchen and casually appointed mudroom.

room would be converted to a formal dining room. And the grand staircase would be cleaned, restored, and made to look as regal as it did in the 1890s, when it would have impressed even the most stately visitors. But moving from the front of the house to the rear, Treff reconceived every space: Small rooms would be opened up and interior views expanded, informality would replace formality, and the kitchen would no longer be the domain of domestic help but rather the hub of the house, where family and friends could gather and entertain.

Treff passed his design on to Tom Silva, and work began on the kitchen, of course, since it was in need of the most help. The crew took down walls, put up a new ceiling, installed new windows and doors, and stripped the back staircase that once emptied into the old, small kitchen. With its plaster walls replaced by wooden balusters, this formerly dark staircase, once an afterthought, became

BELOW LEFT: Every inch of the front staircase balustrade was restored, a painstaking process, given its size and many details.

BELOW RIGHT: Victorian kitchens were once reserved for the domestic help, but this one is the centerpiece of the home. This kitchen desk and the mudroom beyond keep the family organized. The front staircase balustrade inspired the gracious sweep of the desk's knee wall.

the main point of entry to the new heart of the house. Treff designed and Tommy built a transparent balustrade that allowed views of the kitchen from the family room, and a view from the kitchen of people coming and going through a side door on the porch. The redesigned staircase made a bold statement: The goings-on in the kitchen would no longer be hidden, and all were invited to join.

For more than a century, the back of the house had been completely disconnected from the yard. Except for a single basement door, the back façade was a three-story wall with few windows and no access to the land. That all changed when Tommy added a large back porch with two separate doors, one into the kitchen and one into a new mudroom that became the home's primary entrance. Out back we added a staircase as wide and graceful as the home's other staircases, which led to a new bluestone patio built by Roger Cook and his crew. The design was clean and sophisticated, with sharp lines and rectilinear forms that set off the house's softer shapes, such as bay windows and flared porch posts wrapped in layers of shingles.

ABOVE: The family room is a transitional space between old and new; the original gas fireplace and oak surround were re-stored, but we paint-ed the room's oak wainscoting white to complement the kitchen. We widened a narrow doorway between the family room and kitchen to create a more open floor plan.

PREVIOUS PAGE LEFT: The large, sweeping staircase that fills an over-sized entry hall is a distinctive feature of shingle-style houses. Walking through the front door and past the stained and leaded glass leaves no doubt about the style of home you've entered.

PREVIOUS PAGE RIGHT: Despite the modern upgrades, this bathroom has a scale and details that give it a vintage feel. Note the faucet coming out of the wall just above the tub.

TOP: We restored all of the stained- and leaded-glass windows, even casting new fleurs-de-lis to replace missing ones.

BOTTOM: The fieldstone retaining wall is interrupted by a built-in bench, an elegant and clever way to add seating without taking up precious patio space.

FACING PAGE TOP LEFT: The previous owners left this pool table in the house. It was a classic, so we had it restored. The lamp above is a dual-fuel antique that once ran on both gas and electricity before people knew which type of fuel would prevail.

FACING PAGE TOP RIGHT: An original cast-iron, claw-footed tub was reconditioned on-site.

FACING PAGE BOTTOM: New balusters for the back staircase provide views to and from the kitchen.

The patio was great for seating and entertaining but did nothing for the boys' baseball games. Unlike Paul and Maddy's previous piece of property, which was flat and expansive, this backyard sloped away from the house steeply and quickly. Paul described it as a "ski slope," and the idea that his boys might never play in the yard concerned him so much that he almost talked Maddy out of buying the home several times. The solution? A tiered backyard. The bluestone patio was the upper tier, directly connected to the kitchen via the short staircase and new entryway to a recently finished basement. A fieldstone wall, also capped in bluestone, surrounded the patio and separated it from the lower tier, a large and flat lawn. Creating flat ground where a "ski slope" once existed required lots of earth-moving and a new retaining wall, although this one was made from concrete block since it couldn't be seen from the house. The lower half of the yard was now flat and big enough for a decent Wiffle ball game, and that delighted Paul and his boys.

The architect knew it didn't make sense to reconfigure the *entire* house— that wasn't what the homeowners wanted. The shingle-style form was so pronounced in this quintessential Victorian that a complete update risked putting the home in conflict with itself. It did make sense, however, to preserve

TOP LEFT: The old foyer was elegant but cold. We added insulation underneath, a new heating system, and closet space, which would have been novel ideas to the Victorians.

TOP RIGHT: The front living room is the most formal room in the house, made more so by the designer's choice of a symmetrical layout. The three bay windows overlook the expansive front porch. The antique clock in the corner is one of dozens from the homeowner's collection.

FACING PAGE: The kitchen, no longer a warren of small spaces, connects to the rest of the house and is opened to the backyard for the first time. The door to the right of the kitchen table leads to a new covered porch and a spacious patio.

the front of the house in its original state while completely gutting and updating the back of the house. And to ease the transition between these two spaces—between the two eras in the home's evolution—was the middle ground. The new family room sat between the very formal dining room and the pleasantly less formal kitchen. One wall of the family room now features a cast-bronze fireplace with a painted slate surrounding an ornate mantelpiece original to the house, a touchstone of the Victorian era. But on the other three walls, the rich oak wainscoting that had been preserved throughout the rest of the house was covered over with a fresh and contemporary coat of white paint, as if to mask the home's Victorian origins.

There was an elegant but narrow pocket door on the front of the family room, while the back of the family room was connected to the kitchen with a wide, open

doorway. The entire space was a delightful mix of old and new that eased the transition through a century of upgrades and improvements to the house.

The successful renovation of our 1890s Victorian was full of great lessons on how to make an old home work with a modern lifestyle. What our architect fully understood and our homeowners came to appreciate was that if a house was going to serve two purposes—the preservation of its historic roots and the service of a modern family—it had to have balance. Old and new spaces could not sit next to one another without proper transitions and good flow. Our house, thanks to its architect and Tom's talented crew, flowed seamlessly between its Victorian splendor and the crisp function of a contemporary home. And despite living just a few blocks from their old house, I doubt that Paul and Maddy often return, now that there's plenty of space and a great yard for barbecues and baseball. It was clear that for this family, "move and improve" was the right decision.

FACING PAGE: It is no surprise that the family takes most of their meals here in the kitchen. The designer called for neutral tones and custom cushions to complement the unique bench that Tom and his crew had fabricated.

ABOVE RIGHT: The restored pool table is the centerpiece of this Victorian-style third-floor "man cave."

Close Up

Roger Cook

Several years back, Roger and I were filming at a large indoor garden show, the kind with huge exhibits that have full-size trees and working water features. They're beautiful places and great backgrounds for making TV, but they're crowded, and when you work with a television camera in a crowd you tend to get noticed.

Lots of people came up to us to say hi and shake hands that day. At one point, out of the corner of my eye I caught a glimpse of a woman waving at us—well, at Roger, actually—and trying to get a picture. So I got Roger's attention, and made him turn around and smile for the camera. But she kept waving. So Roger kept smiling. And then we figured it out: She wanted Roger to move! He was standing in front of a fake rock and she wanted a picture of that, not of Roger. It was a hilarious misunderstanding and Roger and I still laugh about it.

With Roger, misunderstandings are sometimes, well, understandable. He works outside all day, covered in dirt, yet goes around easily reciting the Latin names of countless flowers and trees. He's physically imposing but the first guy to get down on his knees and play with your kids. If your spirits are down, he's the one to call and check on you, but he never wants any attention in return. He's the kind of guy who limps around for a year with a bum hip because he's too busy caring for others to care for himself.

That's Roger: selfless, dependable, strong. And no one who knows Roger would ever bother to take a picture of a fake rock when the real thing is standing right there.

08. TEXAS BUNGALOW

Texas is hot. Texas is dry. And Texas is tough, at least when it comes to green building. Austin, Texas, has the oldest and toughest green building program in the country, so that's where *This Old House* went to prove our green credentials. Over the course of six months, we worked on our most comprehensive sustainable renovation ever. We turned out all the tricks: recycled materials, alternative energy, efficient heating and cooling systems, rainwater collection, and our secret weapon—a local builder who would make it all happen. We needed to renovate a house and increase its square footage by 50 percent while decreasing its energy use by 50 percent. Texas was hot, dry, tough—and a terrific challenge.

BEFORE

LEFT: Extending the home's original roof line only six feet allowed us to add a second floor without drastically increasing the scale of the building. The second rake board to the left of the chimney is the old roof line.

FACING PAGE: The master bedroom will sit in this small addition off the back. We added just 750 square feet to the house; the homeowners wanted only as much space as they absolutely needed.

It may seem odd that we felt the need to prove our green credentials. For nearly three decades, the team at *This Old House* has built with sustainability and energy efficiency in mind. Yankee thrift, which is part of our team's DNA, is the very definition of sustainable: It stands for building only what you need and wasting even less. Norm Abram, our first general contractor and current master carpenter, was famously chosen for those roles because his job-site scrap pile was always so small. And long before anybody was counting BTUs, carbon footprints, or points for green certification, our guys, led by plumbing and heating contractor Richard Trethewey, were talking about the weather-responsive controls, heat-transfer coefficients, and super-efficient heating and cooling systems that Richard discovered on his travels around the world.

But there's always more to be done. In 2007, "green" was on the tip of everyone's tongue. The ENERGY STAR labels found on appliances were now slapped on homes, too. Big houses were out and not-so-big ones were in. There were books, conferences, television shows, and entire television networks dedicated to living green. We were even told that if we all "greened" our homes we might solve the inconvenient problems that have placed our planet in peril. So despite having practiced for three decades what others were now preaching, we decided to "go green"—officially—and renovate a home according to the guidelines of the oldest and strictest green building program in the country.

The city of Austin developed its green building program in 1992. It was the first municipal program of its kind and preceded other programs like ENERGY STAR and LEED (Leadership in Energy & Environmental Design). It was also one of the toughest—fewer than .5 percent of the 6,000 homes rated by the program have qualified for its elite, five-star rating. We knew five stars wouldn't come easily but we were confident the team we put together and the house we chose would mean success.

Our house was a 1926 bungalow in the Hyde Park neighborhood of Austin, a leafy enclave just a few miles from downtown. Michele Grieshaber bought the house in 1997 and lived there alone until 2007, when she married Michael Klug, who moved in with his two young sons. The 1,500-square-foot house, with two bedrooms and one bathroom, provided plenty of space for Michele but was too small for a family of four. A renovation and small addition were in order.

FACING PAGE, TOP: The new master bedroom will have a vaulted ceiling, a wall of windows, and a new deck.

FACING PAGE, INSET: We installed a rainwater collection system, including this steel tank in the backyard. The drought-tolerant plants and tiny patch of grass won't need much irrigation.

TOP LEFT: We completely removed the old kitchen so we could open the space to the rest of the house and to the backyard. The homeowners wanted to "live outside" as much as possible, despite the scorching Texas heat.

TOP RIGHT: Just about every building material in the house is sustainable or recycled. The new wood floors came from old beams from a New England mill building, and the door in the background came from a local salvage yard; it perfectly matched the home's existing doors.

AFTER

The home, full of period bungalow details, was nicely proportioned and well positioned on its corner lot. But in spite of the obvious need for more space, Michele was terrified of a renovation that could ruin everything she loved about her charming "antique." After a long search for the right contractor, a friend pointed her toward Bill Moore, insisting he was "the only one who knew how to work on these old houses." And, in fact, Bill *had* worked on a lot of old houses—nearly forty in Hyde Park alone. But Bill is more than just a prolific builder. He was also one of the first practitioners of green building in the country. In fact, the first house ever rated by the first certified green building program in the United States was one of Bill's. Built in 1992, it received Austin's highest rating at the time.

With Bill on board and drawings from the architect in hand, work got under way. The plan was to add a second story with two bedrooms, a second bathroom, and a small office space, then renovate the kitchen and add a new screened-in porch off the back of the first floor. All of this needed to fit into only 750 new square feet, and under a new roof line that was only six feet higher than the original. Keeping the home small was essential to making it energy efficient, and Michael and Michele were committed to adding only the space they needed.

FACING PAGE: The homeowners didn't want any more space than absolutely necessary, so the new second-floor bathroom is shared by the master and guest bedrooms. The countertops and tub surround are made of recycled glass.

TOP LEFT: Despite the addition of the second floor, the height of the home increased by only six feet, ensuring that the house would still fit into the neighborhood and not overwhelm the lot.

TOP RIGHT: A wall of windows in Texas requires something to keep out the hot sun. In the master bedroom, we used shutters to cover all of the glass, including the door.

ABOVE: A reflective metal roof with lots of insulation beneath it is the best way to keep a Texas house cool in the summer. Thanks to this roof (and its insulation), the home's electric bill, including air conditioning, averages a mere $25 a month.

FACING PAGE: Making rooms do double duty keeps a house small and efficient. The landing at the top of the stairs also serves as library, reading nook, and office.

Despite our goal to "green" the house and secure Austin's coveted five-star rating, there was plenty of traditional renovating and restructuring to do. The house had no foundation and instead rested on a matrix of beams attached to a series of piers sunk into the ground beneath the house. The soil was full of clay—"Texas gumbo," they call it—and during Austin's brief rainy season it swelled and lifted the piers, sometimes unevenly, under the house. Then, during the long, hot summers and drought season that followed the rain, the soil dried out, shrank, and caused the piers to drop unevenly. As a result, the house heaved and sank, season after season, year after year, causing plaster to crack and windows and doors to wrack and stick. With no green points on the line, Bill installed a network of screw jacks under the house and used them to raise or lower the first floor until the house was level. He also installed a bladder system around the perimeter of the house to regulate the soil's moisture, keeping the ground dry in the rainy season and wet in

the summer, thus reducing the swelling and shrinking of the Texas gumbo. As an added precaution, several of the screw jacks were left in place so the homeowners could re-level the house as needed.

When it comes to renovation, the word "green" can refer to many things: energy use, air quality, recycling, or sustainability; in this case, it referred to all of those and more. Bill, who takes a comprehensive approach to his renovations, started with deconstruction, the process of picking apart the house and recycling some materials while reusing others. Old roof rafters removed to make way for the new second-story addition were re-milled on-site and turned into moldings and a balustrade for the new staircase. The new wood floors came from old beams formerly in a New England mill building. The interior doors and hardware came from a salvage yard. The framing lumber was made up of scraps of

FACING PAGE: From the new deck off the master bedroom you can see the deep roof overhangs that help shade the house. Hand-made red-painted screens add charm and a pop of color.

ABOVE: The homeowners asked for nine different colors in the kitchen and chose a green-glass backsplash to complement the recycled glass countertops.

old two-by-fours finger-jointed and glued together to make sufficient lengths. Even the new countertops in the kitchen and upstairs bathroom were made from recycled liquor bottles. And if the material wasn't recycled, chances were it was sustainable. The kitchen cabinet frames were made from fast-growing Lyptus wood, while the cabinet boxes were built from medium density fiberboard (MDF)—scraps of lumber converted into wood flour and reconstituted into sheets. Recycled and sustainable materials were everywhere.

Recycled materials also helped with our goal to make the house energy efficient. We stripped off the dark asphalt roof and replaced it with a metal one. Metal is infinitely recyclable and will last several times as long as the asphalt, but most important, its light color could reflect the heat of the hot Texas sun and help keep the house cooler, reducing air-conditioning (and thus, electricity) use. We filled the walls with cellulose insulation— effectively, recycled newspaper—that helped with both the summer heat and chilly winter nights. But materials could take us only so far in our effort to reduce energy consumption; the mechanical equipment would have to do the rest.

We started with simple ideas like an on-demand water heater that only used fuel to make hot water when it was needed, instead of continuously warming a forty-gallon tank every hour of every day. The air-conditioning equipment was upgraded from a ten-SEER (seasonal energy efficiency ratio) unit to a sixteen-SEER unit, a dramatic leap in efficiency. But most important, we moved these systems—the water heater and air-conditioning ducts—into the insulated and conditioned space of the house. This reversed the existing poorly designed system, which had forced cold, conditioned air through an uninsulated attic that could get as hot as 180 degrees in the summer, and required the

FACING PAGE: The guest bedroom best shows off the new roof line. Placing windows all the way to the peak of a room makes a dramatic statement on both the inside and the outside of the house.

ABOVE: Handmade forged-metal sconces and small triangular windows are just some of the details that keep the bungalow charm of the house.

RIGHT: The family uses the new screen porch nine months out of the year. The builder custom-made the screen frames so they'd match the rest of the home and used Ipe for the decking. Ipe's toughness has earned it the nickname "ironwood."

water heater to make and store hot water in the same attic, which could drop to thirty-five degrees in the winter.

Some of the systems we installed saved energy and some systems *made* energy, like the solar panels we easily clipped to the standing-seams of our new metal roof. The rooftop photovoltaic panels were sized to generate 2.4 kilowatts of power, or about half of the family's estimated needs, and thanks to the roof's good southern exposure and some healthy rebates from Austin's electric utility, the panels were not only effective—they were affordable.

Bill will tell you he never "plays for points," and it's easy to believe when you see his team in action. No one on his crew kept a running log of how many green points they gained or lost when they used the plastic material from old highway billboards as tarps to cover their lumber, or when his carpenters sifted through scrap piles for the right size of two-by-four instead of cutting a new one to length. Bill made no distinction between building green and building well. But there was an "official" tally, and when the job was complete we got our score. In the end, the renovation not only earned Austin's five-star rating but also garnered more points than any previous renovation in the program's history. And of all the renovations ever rated by Austin's

ABOVE: The kitchen seating area is flanked by the screen porch and a small room for watching television. The homeowners wanted the bookcases to pop, so we painted them a rich red inspired by chile peppers.

ABOVE: Screens block nearly half of the airflow through an opening, so a screen porch built around double French doors is a good way to get cool breezes into the house on a hot summer day.

Green Building Program, only three had received five-star ratings. Bill Moore could now be credited with two of those projects.

But beyond that, we delivered the homeowners a well-designed, properly built house that was comfortable, healthy, and efficient. I visited with Michele and Michael four years after we completed the renovation and listened to them talk about how much they loved and used their new home. As we sat comfortably in the kitchen on a ninety-degree day in March, cooled by the breezes flowing from the screen porch, we saw the most dramatic results in the form of the family's electric bills. While their neighbors were spending as much as $300 to $500 a month to run their air conditioning in the summer, Michele and Michael's highest electric bill was $89—in August! Their electric bills averaged about $25 a month, and in some months they were net *producers* of electricity, sending excess kilowatts back to the grid.

So what is a "green" renovation? Well, I'm not sure I could come up with a single definition, but I would point to our Austin project as a perfect example: Use only the materials you need, be conscious of where they come from and where the waste goes, create a healthy living environment, and know you're on the right track if you can build a bigger house that uses *less* energy. It's a formula that *might* win you five stars, but will always mean a better house.

LEFT: The newly opened kitchen communicates better with the rest of the house. We added cabinets to the wall between the kitchen and dining room to add storage but also to give the wall depth and character.

RIGHT: A small desk is tucked into the new wall cabinets, facing the kitchen. Every space in a small home must serve multiple purposes.

BELOW: Over the years the home had settled several inches; this chimney was the low point. The builder used screw jacks under the house to re-level the floor, leaving a few behind so the homeowners could make adjustments as needed in the future.

Close Up

Bill Moore

Bill Moore has impeccable green-building credentials. He built the first house for the first green-building program in the United States—in Austin, Texas—and he has received more top ratings for renovations than any other builder in that program's history. In addition to being accomplished and smart, Bill is also one of the hardest-working builders around, and when it came to our Austin project, Bill gave everything he had—right down to the hammer on his hip.

Bill fell in love with building early in his life. When he was five, his father built the family a playhouse; Bill was enthralled. At fourteen, he built his sister a stall for her horse; it was his first project, and it stood for three decades. And when he graduated from college with a degree in biology but little opportunity for a good job in his chosen field, Bill fell back on his carpentry skills and joined a framing crew to help pay the bills.

He joined the crew bringing his extensive experience and enthusiasm for carpentry—and carrying a new hammer. It was a twenty-two-ounce Bluegrass framing hammer with a waffle head and a unique octagonal wooden handle. The handle's eight facets kept the hammer square in his hand, and when he hit a nail just right, the steel head made a distinctive ping, a reassuring sound Bill heard continuously for forty years.

But the hammer, sadly, was silenced on our Austin project, lost underneath the new staircase, perhaps, or entombed in the attic insulation. That hammer is an apt metaphor for all that Bill gave to our project: forty years of experience and enthusiasm, an innovative approach to building that is just now attaining recognition in this country, and the reassurance that building green really means building *smart*.

09. SPANISH REVIVAL

There are many things that draw people to Los Angeles: the sunny weather, miles of beaches and boardwalks, and, of course, the bright lights of Hollywood. But in typical *This Old House* fashion, we weren't drawn by any of those things. For us, it was about the architectural styles that are hard to find in New England and a curiosity about where the Angelenos who work in America's second-largest city actually make their homes. So despite four previous visits to California, the cast and crew of *This Old House* packed up and headed west again, this time to Los Angeles, for the first time in the show's history. When we got there we found just what we were looking for.

BEFORE

LEFT: This is the home's original kitchen. It was quaint but tiny—so small that the refrigerator and dishwasher had to go in a separate room.

FACING PAGE: Everybody loved the original bathroom tiles, a quintessential feature of the 1930s Los Angeles bungalow, but the bathroom shower leaked, and the floor underneath was rotted away, so the tiles had to go.

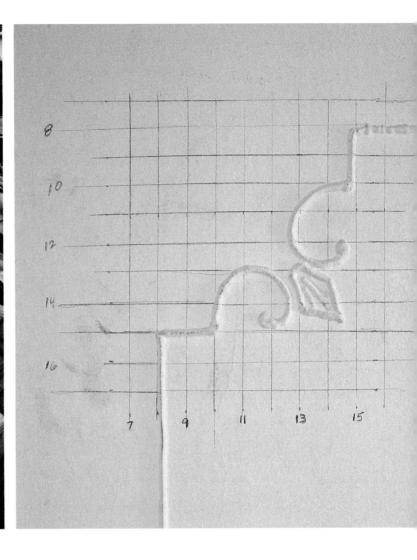

It was a Spanish Colonial Revival house in a Los Angeles neighborhood called Silver Lake, home to Kurt Albrecht and his wife, Mary Blee. The house had all the distinctive features one would expect from a Spanish Colonial: a red-clay tile roof, warm stucco walls, arches and ornamental iron work adorning both the entryway and the large picture window out front. The house was built in 1933 at a time when Silver Lake was an up-and-coming neighborhood, home to many people who worked in the film industry, and the place where Walt Disney built his first studio. Silver Lake was also known for its healthy mix of iconic California housing—the Spanish Colonial and Mediterranean-style homes, as well as a variety of mid-century modern dwellings. Its proximity to downtown Los Angeles,

Hollywood, and many of the major studios in Culver City and Glendale made it a favorite neighborhood of hard-working Angelenos.

Silver Lake, and this house in particular, first attracted Kurt back in 1988. He bought the home in his bachelor days but married a few years later, and a few years after that, Mary gave birth to a daughter. But the house was small—only fifteen hundred square feet—with two bedrooms and a single bath. The kitchen was so tiny that the refrigerator and dishwasher had to be stored in an adjoining room. The house had blemishes, too. Its only shower leaked so badly that it was unusable, so Kurt had rigged a temporary shower in the stand-alone tub. When we arrived in the summer of 2010, the "temporary" shower had been in service for nearly a decade.

AFTER

But despite its flaws and small size, it was easy to see why Kurt and Mary loved the house. It sat up on a hill overlooking the Silver Lake Reservoir, which not only gave their neighborhood its name but also gave the house water views. Its proximity to work was also appealing: Both our homeowners worked in film production—Kurt for Sony and Mary for DreamWorks—and their respective studios were only a few miles away. But more than anything, Kurt and Mary loved the home's charming details.

The house, situated on a small lot, fit snugly into the neighborhood. Its front sat low to the ground and was only one story tall, but the arched entryway, complete with its iron gate, was welcoming. Inside, the arches were repeated in the openings between rooms, and the mahogany casing around these Moorish doorways was complemented by original hardwood floors with decorative inlays. The kitchen was quite attractive, despite its tiny size, with warm yellow wall tiles running from countertop to ceiling, and two bright windows flanking an enamel-coated cast-iron kitchen sink. The dining room opened onto a breezy

FACING PAGE: The front of the house received some new ornamental ironwork and an updated coat of stucco with a new paint color integrated. We landscaped the front yard and made a front walk out of broken slabs of concrete playfully called "urbanite." I was skeptical at first, but liked the finished look.

TOP LEFT: We added two balconies: one off the master bedroom upstairs and a second off the first floor bedroom (shown here). Between the sweeping stucco forms underneath and the iron railings, it was easy to imagine our home as a Spanish villa.

TOP RIGHT: The homeowner and his father had built a small deck off the dining room. We replaced it with this courtyard, which is also accessible from a new guest bedroom on the first floor.

patio, and one of the bedrooms featured a Juliet balcony overlooking the small backyard. Art deco sconces hung throughout the house and the bedroom walls had a simple yet elegant plaster detail known as "cake frosting," a name derived from the unique process used to apply it to the walls: A cook's pastry bag was filled with wet plaster, and a craftsman would apply small beads by hand around the perimeter of the room, taking time to add small flourishes in the corners.

But the most distinctively Los Angeles feature of the house was probably the bathroom—and I'm not talking about its leaks. The room had a mix of quintessentially West Coast tiles with rich yellow walls, deep greens on the floor, a black border around the entire room, and even more yellow and green tiles on the vanity countertop. To complete the effect, the tub and toilet were— dare I say it—an avocado green. Kurt and Mary loved all the details and were committed to saving or replicating as many of them as possible.

The plans for the renovation were driven primarily by the need for more space. What was once a bachelor pad was now home to Kurt, his wife, their daughter, and a baby on the way. Two bedrooms and a single bath would not suffice for a family of four; the plan was to add two new bedrooms, another bathroom, and a half-bath. Given the small lot—the neighboring houses sat only about twelve feet away on either side—we decided to build up, adding a second

PREVIOUS PAGE, LEFT: The fireplace was one of the original features that caused the homeowners to fall in love with the house. Some plaster repair and new paint were all it needed from us.

PREVIOUS PAGE, RIGHT: The designer played up the Spanish flair of the house. The Moorish arch in the picture window set the tone, and she chose the décor accordingly.

BELOW LEFT: This "cake frosting" detail in the master bedroom was applied by hand; the imperfect lines are deliberate.

BELOW RIGHT: The new railings and all the ornamental ironwork are a combination of hand-wrought and prefabricated pieces.

floor to the back of the house but leaving the front nearly untouched, to keep its low profile and to ensure that it still fit within the neighborhood.

In total, we added about seven hundred and fifty square feet. In addition to the new space, we updated the tiny kitchen and leaky bathroom. We converted the first-floor bedrooms into a family room, nearly tripled the size of the kitchen, which now opened easily onto the living space, and added a new staircase to the second floor. But the most dramatic new feature was the back terrace. Two large doors, flanked by floor-to-ceiling windows, opened onto a new patio featuring terra-cotta tiles underfoot and handmade iron railings around its perimeter. Two new Juliet balconies were added off the bedrooms, and for the first time in its history the house was properly connected to its small but inviting yard. A second floor was added with a proper master suite and a second room that would serve as the nursery for a few

years and then be converted to a home office when the new baby moved to one of two new first-floor bedrooms. We updated the mechanical systems for comfort and efficiency, adding central air and a new heating system (enclosed in an insulated space for the first time). We also updated the windows throughout the entire house. Surprisingly, the new windows featured only a *single* pane of glass containing a highly reflective coating, instead of double-paned glass and its insulating properties. This choice was a stark example of how hot the California sun can be and the lengths a good builder will go to keep the radiant heat out of the house.

Our local contractor, Los Angeles–based Home Front, did the work for us. They specialize in the restoration and reproduction of old homes and are very familiar with distinctive West Coast styles. Their diverse crew included an art historian, a former jeweler (now in charge of hardware restoration), a cerebral son of Princeton University professors, and a long list of hardworking Mexican-American craftsmen and job bosses who kept the mood light and who could be found laughing with one another just as hard as they worked.

This was just the kind of diverse and multitalented crew the house needed. One day they poured a reinforced foundation able to withstand the forces of earthquakes and the unique stresses felt by buildings on steep hillsides; the next day they showcased old-world crafts like troweling stucco or worked with seventy-year-old clay roof tiles. These tiles, found on the roof originally, were handmade by craftsmen in Mexico who bent wet slabs of clay over their thighs to give the tile its curved and tapered profile, then dragged their fingers across the wet tile to make its distinctive ridges. Each tile was unique and filled with character, but they were so precious and so expensive to re-create that our crew was forced to use new tiles on the roof of the new addition. To preserve the beautiful look of the original roof, the new tiles were only installed in the field, which couldn't be seen from the ground, while the old tiles, harvested from the existing roof, were cleverly placed around the perimeter. Despite about three hundred square feet of new, simpler tiles, the roof still looked original and untouched.

PREVIOUS PAGE, LEFT: From the street it is hard to see the second-story addition, except from this spot, just over the garage roof. An iron-covered niche breaks up the gable-end wall of the addition.

PREVIOUS PAGE, RIGHT: The new master bedroom is smaller than the one the home-owners gave up but much improved, with two French doors leading to the balcony. The bedroom shares the same plaster cove-and-tray ceiling detail found throughout the first floor.

BELOW: We used hand-painted reproduction tiles with colors and designs inspired by the famous and much-coveted Malibu tiles that were first manufactured not far from our house.

The crew was able to preserve or re-create many other original details that Kurt and Mary loved. They rewired and rehung the original art deco sconces. The wood floors, with their Moorish inlay, were repaired and refinished in some rooms and replicated in others. We couldn't save the original bathroom tiles, with their distinctive yellows and greens, but they were reproduced by hand, and the addition of a whole new palette of retro colors made the new spaces—the kitchen and bathrooms—feel as authentic and vibrant as the original house.

As is often the case, our adopted Los Angeles crew squeezed about eleven months of work into six months without sacrificing quality or attention to detail, and as the project was coming to a frenetic conclusion in January, Mary gave birth to a son. About two months later the entire family returned to their new home—expanded, updated, and newly efficient, but still as charming and authentic as it was when it was built back in 1933.

ABOVE LEFT: A far cry from the original, the new kitchen even has enough space for luxuries like a wine refrigerator.

ABOVE RIGHT: The plaster cove-and-tray ceiling detail is obvious here in the dining room. The detail was replicated throughout the house by a skilled plasterer and with the help of foam molds.

ABOVE: The designer believes large furniture makes a small room feel bigger. The tall bedposts here have the effect of raising the ceiling. Their heavy, dark turnings are squarely in the Spanish style.

ABOVE: The kitchen is now three times its original size, which may be the homeowners' favorite feature. But my favorite is the plaster cove that wraps into the upper cabinets and makes them feel integrated with the wall. Even the stainless-steel range hood was plastered over, and small corbels under the cabinets give the entire room an Old World, Spanish feel.

Close Up
Angel Leon

At seventeen years of age, Angel Leon arrived in Mexico City and was greeted like a conquering hero. People carried his bags, drove him around, and even asked for his autograph. He had just been recruited to pitch for a professional baseball team, and he happily left his native California to pursue his boyhood dream. "From zero to hero in a four-hour flight" is how he described the experience.

Six months later, he broke his arm in an accident, and Angel's baseball career was over. He returned to California to look for a job—this time carrying his own bags. He tried working in a factory and sitting behind a desk, but nothing seemed to take. The inside work, he said, made him feel like a caged animal, so he decided to go into construction. He got to work outdoors, he loved the camaraderie with the crew, and he also had a special skill—at just seventeen, Angel could read construction drawings. At fourteen, he had seen his first plan in his family's garage, where his father and friends gathered nightly to shoot pool. Many of the older men worked in construction and saw young Angel's interest in the rolled-up documents that always seemed to be at their sides. They taught Angel to read the plans and soon he was on his way. And that was our good fortune.

Twenty-seven years later, we asked Angel and his L.A. crew to compress eight months of work on our Silver Lake project into five. It was a challenge, but he pulled his team together masterfully, and they finished the job precisely on time. On the last hectic day before our wrap party, I caught a glimpse of Angel's crew on cleanup duty, hauling garbage bags, unused bags of concrete, and tool bags. And Angel, once again the conquering hero but still every bit the team player, happily carried a few bags himself.